s going to die I have traveled

them in incredible detail, det

e exact date) of many signific

empts, and the like I have

negotiations I have revealed to private ii.

ight, and even hair color of unborn children, business

n combat in Vietnam, for instance) I have relived crimes

rits—persons later arrested and convicted for the crime

pecially children I have diagnosed illness before it was

thing from stolen sports cars to misfiled receipts I have

their owners I have relayed important information from

ve knowledge of some sort, knowledge I couldn't have

ch as clairvoyance, telepathy, precognition, or ESP But

meras of all descriptions—still cameras, movie cameras,

be recorders, and many other kinds of equipment I have

ear that were not visible to the naked eye, or in which

s to go out in rooms, buildings, even an entire town—

out touching them I have projected images onto walls

of light in totally dark rooms I have appeared in front of

have separated one part of my consciousness from the

the surroundings, then returned and reported what I saw

me again, in a scientific laboratory, under tightly con-

, moved an object, then returned—also under carefully

instruments in one room while my physical body was in

"depsyched" houses occupied by poltergeists I have

this world In most cases, I have *precise, documented*

partial witnesses, scientific evidence I have known in

ve traveled backward in time to view past events while

edible detail, detail only an actual observer could have

of many significant events, including wars, explosions,

e like I have foretold with precision the results of elec-

have revealed to private individuals many events in their

en hair color of unborn children, business failures or

bat in Vietnam, for instance) I have relived crimes in

ulprits—persons later arrested and convicted for the

ple, especially children I have diagnosed illness before

everything from stolen sports cars to misfiled receipts

s about their owners I have relayed important informa-

Beyond Coincidence

BEYOND COINCIDENCE

*One Man's Experiences
with Psychic Phenomena*

ALEX TANOUS
with
HARVEY ARDMAN

DOUBLEDAY & COMPANY, INC.
GARDEN CITY, NEW YORK
1976

ISBN: 0-385-11242-4
Library of Congress Catalog Card Number 75–14842
Copyright © 1976 by Alex Tanous
All Rights Reserved
Printed in the United States of America
Book Design by Bente Hamann
First Edition

A Dedication

First, I would like to dedicate this book to my mother and father, with warm and loving memories. Without them, I could have had no psychic life.

Second, I would like to dedicate this book to Mr. and Mrs. Joseph Shamy, good and generous friends, without whom this book would not have been possible.

Acknowledgments

I wish to thank all the people who have so graciously contributed to this book. Without them it would never have been written. I also wish to thank Kay Tacouni, Ann Magid, Mr. and Mrs. Carlton S. Sedgeley, Betsy Beard, Ron Turigliatto, Clara Paoletti, Mable Vinson, Loretta Deveau and Fern Cederberg.

In addition, for their kind permission to reprint previously published material, I would like to thank *The Church World*, Maine's official Catholic weekly; The Energy Research Group of the Institute for Bioenergetic Analysis; *The National Enquirer*; the Utica Observer Dispatch Inc.; the *Maine Sunday Telegram*, the Rumford Falls (Maine) *Times*, the Syracuse *Herald-Journal*, and the Manchester (New Hampshire) *Union Leader*.

Contents

Introduction

When I first met Alex Tanous in spring 1974, I'd just come off a five-year stint as science and technology editor at the Research Institute of America. I was accustomed to seeing and reporting on technological miracles that were not miracles at all, but thoroughly explainable events—achieved not via some special power, but with simple hard work.

In short, I was a convinced skeptic, so far as the psychic phenomena were concerned. I was intellectually and emotionally committed to science and rationality. I can't say now that my association with Alex Tanous has caused me to do a 180-degree flip-flop. One doesn't usually abandon the beliefs of a lifetime overnight. But my pre-Alex view of the world has been thoroughly shaken.

I've now worked with Dr. Tanous over quite a long period. I've talked to dozens of people whose lives have been affected by him, studied stacks of affidavits concerning his psychic accomplishments, closely examined many very strange photographs, and watched him work in scientific laboratories at the American Society for Psychical Research. Time and again, I have been confronted with what —even to my skeptical eye—seems irrefutable evidence of inexplicable doings.

The most disturbing evidence of his powers has come in my personal relationship with him. I have seen him tell people things about their lives he could not possibly have known, merely by holding an object they owned. I have seen him—no other explanation makes sense—"leave his body," "travel elsewhere," "come back," and report on what he's seen. I've seen him predict the future—albeit in small, insignificant chunks—naming cards that would be cut from a deck, before the event.

Just as striking, perhaps, I have seen Alex empower *others* to achieve psychic feats previously totally beyond them. On a number of occasions, under widely differing circumstances, I have seen him "teach" a television newsman to predict which card would come up when he cut the deck, "show" a small child how to "see through" cards—so that she could tell which was red and which was black, *from the back*, "inspire" others to "leave their bodies," somehow "travel elsewhere," then return—with information they could not have possibly obtained sitting where they were. He's even had me doing some of these things, as you will read.

You might wonder why, after what I've seen, I put such expressions as "leave his body," "travel elsewhere," and "come back," among others, in quotation marks. Put it down to my irrational scientific prejudices. It's my way of expressing the conflict I feel when the evidence of my eyes contradicts what I've been taught and what I "believe"—there I go again. I cannot accept it. But I cannot deny it, either.

I feel the same way about some of Alex's even more sensational feats which I did not have the privilege of witnessing (though I find the evidence for them nearly as convincing as if I had been there). From the best information I have—and I've taken *nothing* at face value—Alex has:

· Predicted many events before they happened, some of them international in scope (such as wars, assassination attempts, etc.) and some of them private, even trivial (such as the outcomes of baseball games, the sex and date of birth of unborn children, etc.);

· Performed unexplainable physical feats, such as stopping watches, breaking cameras, turning off the electric lights in a room without touching the switch, projecting visible images *from his eyes*, creating photographable balls of lights in totally dark rooms;

· "Left his body," under rigorous scientific controls, "projected himself" to another room, *moved an object in that room*, and returned.

In the pages that follow, Alex tells of these achievements (and many more), and provides all of the documentary evidence even a skeptic should need—if his mind is open.

I have also seen Alex attempt psychic feats and fail. Strangely enough, this gives me even more confidence in his powers. If he were a magician, he would never fail—since magic tricks are totally under the practitioner's control. But the power Alex has is not totally under his control. It is affected by his mood, by the mood of others around him, by circumstances and by I do not know what else. But when he has it, it is striking.

No introduction of this sort would be complete without a few words about Alex Tanous the man. Perhaps as much as his achievements, his personality and character have persuaded the skeptic in me that he is genuine.

Alex Tanous is one of the kindest, most modest, most unpretentious human beings I have ever known, despite his "unusual abilities." There is absolutely nothing about him of the charlatan or magician. I don't think he'd know how to be dishonest, it's so contrary to his character.

He views his psychic deeds with innocent wonder and delight, almost like an infant taking its first steps. He does not see himself in any way as superhuman, only as fortunate. Further, he is generous with his gifts. He wants nothing more than to share his abilities with those who might benefit by partaking of them. I think these qualities will be evident to anyone who reads this autobiography.

If you are a skeptic, as I am, prepare to defend your beliefs. Or, better yet, open your mind to the thought that there might be more things in this world than you have dreamed of.

If you are a believer, prepare to have your beliefs confirmed and expanded.

Whatever your philosophy, prepare to meet Alex Tanous. I think you'll like him. And I think you'll be impressed.

HARVEY ARDMAN

Beyond Coincidence

My Psychic Journey

Nearly five decades ago I began an incredible journey, a journey of exploration and discovery, a journey of thrills and dangers, a journey into vast unknown and uncharted regions.

This was not an extended survey of strange new lands. Instead, it was an intense internal investigation, a quest for the outmost boundaries of the human mind. It is a quest that has occupied my entire lifetime, a search that continues even now.

This journey has been most often marked by the thrill of discovery and accomplishment. I have found abilities within my mind that far surpass the usual conceptions of the mind's powers. I have performed remarkable psychic feats that have baffled layman and scientist alike. And in truth, I am as baffled as they.

I never cease to be astonished by the growing scope of my psychic skills. Over the years, I've had not only an extraordinary number of psychic experiences, but also an extraordinary variety. And both continue to increase.

For example:

I have known in advance on many occasions that a person was going to die.

I have traveled backward in time to view past events while they were happening, then returned to tell about them in incredible detail, detail only an actual observer could have known.

I have predicted the occurrence (and often the exact date) of many significant events, including wars, explosions, the deaths of important persons, assassination attempts, and the like.

I have foretold with precision the results of elections, horse races, baseball games, and political negotiations.

I have revealed to private individuals many events in their futures, such as marriages, the date of birth, weight, and even hair color of unborn children, business failures or successes, the fate of friends or relatives in danger (in combat in Vietnam, for instance).

I have relived crimes in such detail that I've been able to sketch the faces of the culprits—persons later arrested and convicted for the crime. I've helped police locate many missing or kidnaped people, especially children.

I have diagnosed illness before it was detected by doctors.

I have located lost objects, including everything from stolen sports cars to misfiled receipts.

I have touched objects and from that alone known many things about their owners.

I have relayed important information from departed persons to the living.

Most of these psychic feats involve knowledge of some sort, knowledge I couldn't have gotten in the ordinary way. This kind of knowledge is usually described by terms such as clairvoyance, telepathy, precognition, or ESP. But some of the things I've done go far beyond this.

For example:

I have broken cameras of all descriptions—still cameras, movie cameras, TV cameras—without touching them.

I have stopped watches, tape recorders, and many other kinds of equipment.

I have been the subject of strange photographs, in which things appear that were not visible to the naked eye, or in which things disappear that were visible.

I have caused electric lights to go out in rooms, buildings, even an entire town, simply by willing them out.

I have caused objects to move without touching them.

I have projected images onto walls using nothing more than my eyes.

I have created floating balls of light in totally dark rooms.

I have appeared in front of witnesses in two different places at exactly the same moment.

I have separated one part of my consciousness from the rest, sent it hundreds of miles from my physical body, observed the surroundings, then returned and reported what I saw with total accuracy. And I have duplicated this feat time and time again, in a scientific laboratory, under tightly controlled conditions.

I have left my body, gone into another room, moved an object, then returned—also under carefully controlled conditions. Further, I have been detected by scientific instruments in one room while my physical body was in another.

I have spoken—even battled—with spirits or ghosts and "de-psyched" houses occupied by poltergeists.

I have several times made contact with an energy I believe is not from this world.

In most cases, I have *precise, documented proof* of these acts—tape recordings, affidavits signed by impartial witnesses, scientific evidence. I intend to present all of this in detail in this book.

In addition to my psychic deeds, I have formulated a general theory of the paranormal. Using this theory, I have been able to teach others to duplicate many of my feats.

Though my psychic journey has brought me great fulfillment, it has also brought me persecution and pain. In my youth, I suffered from intense conflicts between my faith—I am a devout Catholic—and my belief in man's psychic powers.

Later, when I refused to renounce this belief, I lost a wonderful job and nearly had my career scuttled. I was denounced from Church pulpits and in the pages of Church newspapers as an agent of the devil.

As I became well known, I saw my personal life disintegrate—when most people (even friends and acquaintances) began to treat me either with fear or awe. They saw me as a god or a devil, or a miracle man. I protested that I was nothing more or less than a normal human being, complete with virtues and faults, but to no avail. Normal relationships became impossible.

More than once, I was on the verge of calling off my quest and rejecting—if I could—my God-given gift. But at the moment of greatest doubt, I was given an extraordinary sign that I should continue with my work, that I should devote myself to it. I came to believe there was a purpose to my unique abilities, even if it had not been made known to me.

Today, I see myself as a kind of pioneer. I am testing, exploring, and discovering a set of abilities all men have, whether they know it or not. I see a host of people following my path, some of whom I am sure will go much farther than I have. I'd like that. I hope someday this will happen with all of humanity.

In a sense, then, my book is a collection of letters sent home from a pioneer, an explorer of strange and wonderful places. It's my contribution to future explorers—an attempt to share my knowledge and my experiences, to warn of the problems and proclaim the pleasures of this particular adventure.

It's my hope that those who take this journey someday will be able to use this book as a guide, so that they may be able to avoid some of the problems I encountered, or know how to overcome them, or at least be prepared for them. It's my hope that future travelers into the psychic realm won't have to begin at the beginning of the road, that my book will give them a head start.

I have a vision for mankind and I pray that what I write here will advance that vision. I see a time when society will encourage its members to practice their psychic abilities. I see a time when throughout human kind, the mind will blossom with new powers.

When that day comes, there will be a new generation of mankind. It will be a psychic generation, but it will be more than that. It will be a generation in which people are truly in touch with one another—and with themselves. It will be a generation in which people will apply their psychic abilities to all of their endeavors.

If this generation comes, it will bring with it the greatest doctors, artists, scientists, businessmen, teachers, and priests of all time. It will truly be the flowering of mankind. I pray that day will come soon.

Come with me now on an incredible journey, a journey into the mind.

The Early Years

Before I was born—even before my parents met—it was predicted that I would have psychic powers.

That prediction came from Kahlil Gibran, the famous Lebanese writer, author of *The Prophet* and many other works. In the early 1920s, he and my father (who was also Lebanese) were friends in New York City. "You will have a son," Gibran told my father, "a man of exceptional gifts, of great abilities—but also a man of great sorrows."

The first confirmation of his prediction came at the very moment of my birth. I was born with what the Middle Eastern people call a "veil." That is, I entered the world with the water bag that protected me in the womb draped over my head and shoulders. In times past, many a child born with a veil suffocated before he could take his first breath. Perhaps for that reason, Middle Eastern tradition holds that the child born with a veil is gifted, that he has what the Western world calls psychic abilities.

And there were other signs. In the palm of my left hand, the creases and folds combined to form a perfect hexagram, or six-pointed star (also known as the Star of David or the Jewish Star). This, too, is accounted a sign of psychic gifts. The famous Dutch psychic, Peter Hurkos, also has a hexagram in his palm. So does Jeane Dixon. Also in my left palm: the mystical cross, a straight vertical line crossed by two short horizontal creases.

Linked to these lines was something even more remarkable—my name, Alex, spelled out backward, quite clearly, in lines and creases. Before I was born, my parents had considered naming me after a grandfather, Alexander. When they saw the palm of my hand, they felt my name had been preordained.

Both the hexagram and my name are plainly visible to this day.

Unlike most American parents, mine were quite willing to accept the unusual circumstances surrounding my birth, and the still more unusual implications. Like my father, my mother was of Lebanese extraction. In fact, all four of my grandparents were Lebanese. The Lebanese people—for that matter, the peoples of the Middle East in general—are especially interested in and concerned with the mystic, the occult, the spiritual, and the psychic, and highly receptive to those who have what they see as divine powers.

Further, both my mother and my father were themselves psychics. Throughout his life, my father gave readings and was a dowser. My mother stayed in the background until he died, then she, too, began to give readings. The family had long known of her psychic abilities, however.

I was born on November 26, 1926, in the family homestead in Van Buren, Maine, in the early morning, as a blinding snowstorm raged outside. My family had come to Van Buren because they felt it resembled their Lebanese home in terrain and climate. In Lebanon, the family had lived in a similar small town.

It is a Middle East custom to use the first name of the father to identify the family, since so many Lebanese last names are the same. My grandfather's father's first name was Tanous (Thomas), and that's what he told immigration officials when he came here. And Tanous it has remained, to this day. But my correct family tree name is Kettaneh. Thus, I am really Alexander Tanous (Kettaneh). My mother's full maiden name was Ann Alice Shalala.

When I was born, the Tanouses were a well-to-do merchant family, owning one of Van Buren's two autos. They sold merchandise door-to-door, carrying it by horse wagon and sleigh. My father, who had some college, was in construction. But the family's financial security would disappear in the Depression, never to return.

It wasn't long after I was born that the signs and portents surrounding my birth were affirmed. The first demonstration of my psychic abilities came at the age of eighteen months. Like all children, I loved the song "Mary Had a Little Lamb." The family had a record of the song, which it kept in and among a stack of perhaps fifty other records. Now it's easy enough for an adult to pick out the record he wants to hear. He flips through them, reading the labels, until he finds the one he wants. But an eighteen-month-old child cannot do this. What I did at that age, according to those who were there, was even more surprising. I felt the *edges* of the records, stopping at one in the middle of the stack and pulling it out. It was "Mary Had a Little Lamb." I did this time and time again, identifying my favorite record by its edge, though no one else could see or feel any difference between the edge of that record and all the rest.

Today, I realize that this was an example of psychometry—knowing something about an object that is apparently unknowable by touching it. I often demonstrate this ability now, at my lectures or on TV shows, touching the edges of a deck of cards, then cutting it to a particular card named in advance. How I do this, I don't know. It just seems natural to me, as it did when I was a baby. Possibly this is because no one ever told me—at least when I was a child—that this was impossible.

As a child, I often saw people visiting my father for a reading. Sometimes, he'd let me watch. My father would take his subject's hand and drop some silver coins through the person's fingers. He felt silver was his conductor, his conduit, that it somehow established contact between himself and his subject.

Then he'd take a deck of ordinary cards and ask the person to cut it. He'd then choose certain cards and begin his reading. He didn't use the cards as a fortuneteller would. Their purpose, he told me, was to serve as a distraction, to relax the subject.

Throughout the reading, he held his subject's hand. And that, he felt, was his secret. That touching contact was the source of whatever information he received about the person. This is psychometry, of course. Today, I use the same technique when I do a reading—minus silver coins, cards, or any other props.

My father did hundreds of readings over the years and became quite well known for his accuracy. Eventually, he attracted devotees from all over the United States and even some other countries.

He never charged for his services. He felt that he had a gift and with that gift came an obligation to share it.

My mother also had a gift. Two events from my childhood demonstrate this without question, I believe. The first occurred in my fifth year. I was playing in the kitchen one day when my mother tripped over me while carrying a big kettle of boiling water. I was drenched in it from head to toe. I vividly remember her picking me up and saying, "Lord, don't let anything happen to this child!" She wiped me off and hugged me to her. Then she took me to a doctor and described what had happened. He was astonished to find that I was neither burned nor scalded. Except for a tiny blister on the back of my neck, I was completely unharmed.

Some psychics attribute their powers to a physical shock like this. I don't think that's true in my case. The signs surrounding my birth, my ability to psychometrically select the record of my choice while still an infant, and, at least one striking instance of precognition (knowing of an event before it happens) before the boiling-water incident, make me think I was born with my powers.

The precognition took place at the age of four. While I was playing with some neighborhood children, I told one of them that he was going to be very sick. The child told his mother what I'd said and she was naturally very upset. She demanded an explanation from my parents, they later told me, and all they could say was that I'd made such remarks before and I'd been right. A few days after I had warned my playmate of his coming illness, he fell sick. Soon after, he died.

Even before I could be disturbed by this, my father reassured me, telling me of similar things that had happened to him. For that reason, I saw nothing unusual about my ability to foretell future events—at least in my early years. I thought everybody had that ability. I still do, for that matter, though I realize few people are in touch with this aspect of themselves, probably because they didn't receive the early encouragement and support that I did.

My personal safety was also involved in the second time my mother demonstrated her powers. And this time, my brothers were also shielded. (I'm the oldest of eight brothers.) At the time, we lived in an apartment over a large garage. One Sunday, after my brothers and I came home from church, we changed our clothes in our rooms and made ready to go outside to play. We headed for the front door, which opened up to a long stairway leading down to the ground.

"No!" My mother shouted, fear in her voice. "Don't go that way."

"Why?" one of us asked.

"Use the back door," she said, not answering the question.

As we walked out the back, the entire *front* of the garage—including the stairway—collapsed. If we had gone that way, we all would have been killed. Later, when I talked to my mother about this, she just said, "I knew what was going to happen. I had a feeling."

Looking back, I realize that there were many things about my childhood that were unusual, though it didn't seem that way at the time. For example, I had what I now recognize as my first out-of-body experience at the age of five. By "out-of-body," I mean that some part of me splits off from the rest of me, some segment of my consciousness, my self, my energy.

At that age, I often amused myself by jumping down a long stairway. I know many children today who enjoy themselves the same way. But two things about my jumping were different. First, I didn't fall, I floated. When I hit bottom, the impact was gentle, as if I weighed no more than a balloon. Now I know dreams of this sort are commonplace. But this was no dream. Second, when I landed, I would look back up the stairs. And there, at the top, would be my "other self," an exact copy of me, naked, ghostlike. I was in both places simultaneously.

This "other self"—I can think of no better description—became my playmate. Even now, I vividly recall waving to him and watching him wave back. I remember talking with him, though I heard his voice inside my head, not through my ears. Usually, he'd stay at the top of the stairs. But at my request, he would jump off the top step, float down—and merge with me. His ability to merge with me and the fact that he was my exact double convinces me that I was having an out-of-body experience.

Today, I am convinced that many, many children—perhaps the

majority—have experiences of this sort. Adults dismiss these experiences by calling the child's other self "an imaginary playmate." They may even dismiss their own memories on this basis.

At that age, I also had contact with what I now believe were the spirits of dead children. Unlike my "other self," these spirit children were dressed and looked solid, rather than ghostlike. But only I could see them. For a long time, I believed they were real children, until I discovered that they were invisible to others.

My parents heard me talking to these spirit children from time to time and asked me who I was talking to. And I'd describe the spirit children to them. Several times, my descriptions exactly matched the deceased children of close relatives. One time, I found myself playing with a set of spirit twins. When I described them to my parents, they knew exactly who they were—relatives' children who had died at the age at which I saw them, but years earlier. I'd never heard of them, until I "met them."

On one occasion, I found myself playing with another spirit child—a little girl. She told me she desperately wanted a doll. She'd never had one of her own. So I asked my mother for a doll to play with. "Why in the world do you want a doll?" she asked. I told her it wasn't for myself, but for one of my spirit friends. My mother got me the doll and I gave it to my playmate.

Soon after that—I was then about eight—I remember coming to my mother in tears. "What's wrong?" she asked.

"I can't find my other self any more," I said. "And I can't jump down the stairs like I used to. My other friends are gone, too." One more thing had vanished: the doll. We never found it.

The many paranormal experiences I have had since then persuade me that these childhood events were real, not the products of an overactive imagination. I believe that children have an unusual capacity for slipping out-of-body, or through the barriers of time and space that separate us from spirit beings.

This susceptible period, I believe, lasts from ages five to eight in most children. It begins when the child is old enough to distinguish between himself and others. It ends when he begins to accept society's view of reality. When parents are quick to dismiss such experiences in their children, their children quickly lose the capacity for them. Fortunately for me, my parents never told me that what I saw just couldn't be.

It wasn't long after I entered school that my psychic abilities began to manifest themselves in new ways. One day, my third-grade teacher, Miss Henrietta Dionne, began reading a poem to the class. I interrupted her—I don't know why—and finished the poem, although I'd never heard it before. My guess is that she was concentrating on the poem and I was receiving it telepathically. Other times, I would give the answer to an arithmetic problem Miss Dionne was writing on the blackboard—even before she was finished writing it.

At the time, these events weren't very striking to me. I don't even remember giving arithmetic answers in advance. But what I did was evidently quite striking to my fellow students. I was reminded of my arithmetic answers only recently by a former classmate, Theresa Ouellette Tarr. And other classmates confirmed her memory—of events that took place forty years ago!

In the evenings, when I came back from selling newspapers or doing whatever I could to help family finances, I'd often sit at the table with my homework, my father beside me, helping me, and gaze into the flickering flame of the kerosene light.

In my mind's eye I would see all sorts of images—images I now recognize as psychic—in the flames of the lamp. I would see events and actions involving people we knew. Once, in the flames, I saw a neighbor being rushed to the hospital. Another time, I saw a family acquaintance about to be arrested for bootlegging. On another occasion, the flickering flames somehow showed me that a friend would fall while bicycling and break his leg. Also, I saw a boy die in the dentist's chair. And all these things happened.

My frequent premonitions always seemed to follow a period of looking into light—either the kerosene light or the oil lamp, or the sun itself. I didn't gaze into the light for the purpose of receiving visions. I looked only because it gave me pleasures, or incidentally, in the course of ordinary events. And the visions came.

Even now, I often "charge myself" by taking a walk in the bright sunlight, or by looking into bright lights. I know that doctors say no one should ever look directly into the sun, since that can permanently damage the retina. But I've been able to do this since childhood with no apparent ill effects. And, in the lab, some of my best work has been done with two five-hundred-watt lights shining directly into my eyes.

Not long ago, I confirmed some of my childhood memories when talking with some of the teachers who taught me in school. "You were such a daydreamer," they said. "You'd go off for a walk in the middle of the day, then come back and tell us that something was going to happen—and it would! We didn't know what to make of it."

I didn't know what to make of it either. But my father understood. He explained to me that light acted for me as silver did for him—that it brought forth what today we call clairvoyant visions. Partly because we were both psychic, our relationship was extraordinarily close and warm. When I was confused, when I was disturbed, when I was perplexed, my father supported and encouraged me. Most of all, he allowed me to be what I was.

In addition to my parents, there was at least one other person with whom I could share my psychic experiences, an odd character named Indian Bill, who lived next door to us. Indian Bill was a chubby, joyful man—a real Indian—who made baskets for potato pickers. As a child, I spent a lot of time with him and he told me many stories of ghosts and spirits. These stories struck a responsive chord in me, of course. So I began to tell Indian Bill of my visions and premonitions. Like my parents, he accepted them instead of ridiculing me.

In certain respects, my Catholic upbringing encouraged me to practice my psychic talents. I read about the lives of saints and I read the Bible and in both places found many examples of psychic phenomena, apparitions, etc. I felt that if such experiences could happen to saints, then they could also happen to ordinary people. And at that time, I had no reason to think of myself as other than ordinary.

At the age of nine, I had another out-of-body experience, the first since the days of my "other self." Early in November, I woke up in the hospital, after an emergency appendectomy. For some reason, I had no memory of leaving my home and being taken to the hospital.

But, while I didn't remember something I should have, I did

remember something I shouldn't have: the entire operation, in precise detail. When I came out of the anesthesia the next morning, I described the whole thing to my astonished nurse. I told her which doctors and nurses had been in the room and what they had done to me.

I believe there have been some cases of incomplete anesthesia, where patients wake up with dim memories of operations they've undergone while apparently unconscious. But mine is no dim memory. It's vivid to me now, as I write these words. And in this memory, my point of view is not that of a patient on an operating table, but of an observer hovering *above the scene*. I can recall looking at my own unconscious body lying on the operating table below "me."

I now know this was an out-of-body experience. Since childhood, I have had many similar experiences—some in the laboratory, under scientifically controlled conditions. In these experiences, my body remains in one place while some part of me travels elsewhere, observes the surroundings, then returns. Most of the time, that part of me which has traveled elsewhere makes its observations while dangling or hovering in mid-air, near the ceiling.

I realize how preposterous these statements sound to anyone unfamiliar with these phenomena. Believe me, I'm just as astonished as anyone that such things are possible. But they are, and in a later chapter, I'll prove it to you.

The same year I had my appendectomy, when I was nine years old, I made my second death prediction. A friend of the family came to visit one night and I shook hands with him when he arrived.

"Sir," I said, "are you ready to die?" I wasn't very tactful at that age, I'm sorry to say.

"What do you mean?" he asked, naturally taken aback.

I blurted out my premonition. "You're going to be dead within twenty-four hours," I said.

The man laughed.

My father was horrified, both by what I had said and by how I had said it. "What are you saying?" he demanded.

"Dad, I just can't help it. That's what I see."

Our friend shrugged and laughed again, while my father made

apologies for me. Before twenty-four hours had passed, our friend was dead of a heart attack.

At about the same time, I began making constructive use of my psychic abilities in school. My best subject was history, not because I loved it so much—though I did—but because I had a special way of studying for tests. I imagined myself back in whatever era we were working on and relived the actual events.

When I told my teachers how I learned more about history than was in my schoolbook, they insisted I was daydreaming—and talking nonsense. In my adult life, however, I have demonstrated to objective scientists my ability to go back in time and relive past events. But I'm getting ahead of my story.

In July 1937—just four months short of my eleventh birthday—my brother Nolan and I were in town selling newspapers, when I suddenly had another premonition, the most disturbing one of my life.

"Let's go home now," I told my brother. "Something terrible has happened to Dad."

We ran all the way. When we got home, we found that moments before my father had had an accident in the garden. A pole he was sticking into the ground to support some climbing beans had broken in half and the point had gone through his eye.

Six weeks later, my father was dead of a cerebral hemorrhage, a complication of the accident. I didn't realize it then, but the happy days of my childhood had come to an abrupt end.

Years of Conflict

When he died, my father left us $1.28. Like many another family, we had never really recovered from the Depression. Now, our sole source of support was gone. What's more, my mother was pregnant with my seventh brother.

Mother called us all together and told us the hard facts of life. We would have to work, those of us who could. Though we would continue our schooling, of course, we would have to earn money in any way possible. In the past, we'd augmented the family income by doing odd jobs. Now, what we earned would *be* the family income.

And so we went out into the world, in earnest. We sold newspapers, picked potatoes, shined shoes, collected discarded bottles, even scavenged for the coal that fell from passing trains, so we could sell it. Somehow, we made out.

Meanwhile, my psychic experiences continued. I was especially sensitive to approaching illness or death—I still am, in fact. A year after my father died, when I was twelve years old, for the third time in my life, I predicted a person's death. I told one of our acquaintances to avoid driving across the railroad tracks because I had a premonition that a train would smash into his car and kill him.

The man smiled a tolerant smile. I knew he was going to ignore my warning. Sure enough, three weeks later, while driving across the tracks of the Canadian Pacific Railroad at one in the morning, his car was demolished by an onrushing freight train and he was killed instantly.

With my father gone and our family nearly destitute, my mother was deeply concerned by my continuing psychic experiences. It wasn't that she disapproved. Far from it. But she was afraid that my abilities might get the family into more trouble than it was in already.

Van Buren is located on Maine's northern border, just across the river from Canada. Most of its citizens are French-speaking Catholics. In my youth, at least, many were puritanical and Jansenistic. They frowned on frivolity of any sort. They were superstitious in the extreme and many believed in ghosts and the supernatural, but they considered fortunetelling the work of the devil.

Though we were respected members of the community, our Lebanese background, the fact that we belonged to the Maronite Rite (an Eastern Rite Catholic, rather than the Roman Rite Catholic) and my father's reputation for readings had already put distance between us and our fellow townsfolk. Now, my mother feared that if I also became known as a psychic, we might become outcast—at the moment we needed goodwill from the community more than ever.

My mother never told me to stop having psychic experiences or to keep my premonitions to myself. But she did tell me not to go out of my way to appear or act differently from everyone else. Only then did I realize just how unusual I was.

She told me that I must first deal with the hard realities of life, and I must grow up and assume my responsibilities. And so the atmosphere of encouragement that I'd lived with until now began to dry up. Who knows what level of psychic achievement I might have reached if the emotional support for that aspect of me had continued?

My mother's message was: restrain yourself, don't push it. Nothing could have been harder for me. On top of my natural psychic impulses, I'd had years of training with my father. Now I was being asked, in effect, to give up a part of myself. I couldn't understand why, no matter how often or how carefully my mother explained it. I began to have the same feeling I'd had when I lost the ability to see my other self and my spirit playmates.

Soon, I entered high school. Things took a turn for the worse for me there. I attended a public school, where some of the teachers were priests. It wasn't long before I was listening to lectures on moral theology. And as I listened, a chill came over my heart.

According to Church doctrine, whenever I practiced my psychic powers, I was in sin, I was doing evil. If I continued my ways, I was sure to be condemned to hell. Yet it was my nature to be psychic. I could no more turn off the flow of premonitions and psychic images than I could stop breathing.

No priest ever actually told me that I was evil (at least not during my high school days). In fact, one went out of his way to tell me I wasn't, that I was only "a hundred years ahead of my time." But I heard many priests say that the kinds of things I was doing were evil. And when I read their canon law, there was no doubt in my mind that I was committing a sin whenever I had a paranormal experience.

After a while, I began to feel I was the carrier of some sort of plague. I could find no way to honor my religion, take my place in the community, and still be true to myself. Faced with this insoluble problem, I slowly began to withdraw into myself. I became more and more introverted.

Not surprisingly, my grades plummeted. I continued to do well in history—for the usual reasons—and English. But I was promoted from year to year not because I'd mastered the material but because no one knew what else to do with me.

Yet I knew I wasn't stupid. Someone gave me a volume of Shakespeare's plays and I read them again and again, entranced. I quoted from them at the least excuse. I grew to love Shakespeare and I drew strength and comfort from his work, especially from *Hamlet* and *Macbeth*, which abounded with references to the paranormal. At the same time, I retreated further and further into my shell.

For two years, I went deeper and deeper into myself, my isolation and introversion growing steadily. It was as if a dark cloud had fallen over me. I couldn't function. I hardly wanted to live if I couldn't be who I was.

The priests thought my difficulties were caused by my father's death, the family's poverty, and the responsibilities I had to shoulder as eldest son. They made allowances for me, passing me when I should have been failed, withholding criticism when I was unable to participate in normal activities.

But in the confessional, finally, I told one priest the truth. He said my trouble was a hyperactive imagination. "Get involved in your schoolwork and school activities," he told me, "and you'll soon be all right."

Unfortunately, he was wrong.

I several times made the effort to break out of my self-imposed isolation, only to have my psychic nature interfere at the last moment.

For example, on one occasion, I signed up for a debate. The subject, as I recall it, was "Will Lend-Lease Involve the United States in War?" My team was assigned the position that it would.

All went well until the middle of the debate. Then, I suddenly stood up and declared, "On December 8, the newspaper headlines will read WAR DECLARED." The year was 1941. Even now, some of my former classmates remember my prediction and the hush that came over the room when I made it.

I knew that I had another psychic experience, that I had sinned once again. And when my prediction came true, it deepened my depression. I was convinced I was evil.

My psychic self also made itself felt when I was with my friends. Girls I knew began to ask me what would happen to their boy friends in the war. Boys asked me how they would fare in the draft. And I would answer their questions, under the guise of advice. But we all knew there was more involved.

I went to another priest and described my problem. He had no understanding of psychic phenomena, but he told me I was going through a "scrupulous period"—a time of seeing evil where there was no evil. There was nothing that could be done about this, he told me. Eventually, the feeling would fade.

It didn't fade. It got worse, much worse. One spring, I was playing football with my friends, among them a blond, blue-eyed boy named Everett Tilley. I was running with the ball when he tackled me. I went down hard and came up mad. "You're going to die for that!" I shouted at him. Six months later, on November 26—*my birthday*—Everett Tilley died of a ruptured appendix.

Today, I feel that my remark was a simple prediction, based on a premonition. At the time, I was certain I'd caused his death. I went to a priest and told him the whole story, but got no satisfactory answer. He neither condemned me nor reassured me. But I felt condemned. My guilt feelings were almost too much to bear.

As far as the Church was concerned, my psychic experiences could only be explained in one of two ways. Either I was a saint or I was in league with demonic forces. From the Church's point of view, the latter explanation seemed far more likely than the former. That much was obvious from what I'd heard and read of moral theology.

Despite my guilt and confusion over Everett Tilley's death, however, I knew deep inside of me that I was neither saint nor demon. I was a human being, with human needs, human virtues, human flaws. The only thing really extraordinary about me was my psychic power.

By now, I felt I was on the verge of a mental breakdown. I had to resolve my internal conflict one way or another—in favor of my religion or myself and the dictates of my conscience.

In the fall, while I worked in the potato field, picking potatoes by the mile, I wrestled with the problem. This went on for weeks. Finally, I came to a decision. I resolved to do what I felt was right, to act upon my psychic images and premonitions according to the dictates of my conscience.

At the same time, I decided to reduce my commitment to my religion, much as my religion meant to me. I know now that if the conflict had been any greater, I might have given up my religion altogether.

This decision was the first positive action I'd taken for years. In a way, I was reaffirming my obligation not to harm myself. The way I'd been going was certainly self-destructive.

I was convinced that I was neither saint nor demon, but a human being, though a human being with unique abilities. Later, I was to discover that many others had psychic powers, but as a high school boy in Van Buren, Maine, at the beginning of World War II, I had no way of knowing that.

My decision did not end the conflict between my psychic self and my religion. The final resolution didn't come until decades later, after the Church proposed the doctrine of conscience at the Ecumenical Council. This doctrine allowed me to return to Catholicism wholeheartedly, since it let me obey both the tenets of my religion and my own conscience.

It was to be a long journey back for me until I had regained the comfort with my psychic abilities and the self-confidence I'd had in my early years. But at least my decision ended the tailspin.

One of my confessions in this period was to a young Marist priest, Rev. Arthur Duhamel, S.M., whom I greatly admired. It was not a happy experience. I knew that he intended to go to Guadalcanal shortly. As I talked to him, another premonition came over me. "Don't go overseas," I told him. "If you do, you'll never see America again. You'll be killed, bayoneted through the throat. And your church will be burned to the ground."

He took my warning gravely, but with no comment. And he left as scheduled. On October 14, 1942, he was bayoneted through the throat and killed, along with two nuns. The three of them were buried near the remains of the church.

Before I left high school, I was given a helping hand by one of the other priests, Rev. Elorge Laplante, the teacher in one of my shop classes. He was talking about electricity when he made an off-the-cuff remark that had a great effect on how I saw my abilities.

"If you could throw yourself into a distant light wave," he said, "I imagine that you could see exactly what had happened when the light wave was born."

I thought about what he said. Somehow, it seemed to apply to me. After all, I had always had a strange relationship to light, beginning with the flickering flames of the kerosene lamp on our kitchen table. Also, I had the inexplicable ability to travel backward in time, to relive past events. Perhaps that ability and my relationship to light were linked in some way.

Father Laplante and I talked about this, but were able to come to no conclusions. Of all the priests I knew in high school, however, he was the most sympathetic and helpful. Later, he tutored me in algebra and geometry so that I could get into college.

My college career did not begin until nine years after I graduated from high school, however. First came a stint in the Army, at Fort Bragg, North Carolina.

Because of my unusual sensitivity to death, the time I spent in the service was probably the most difficult of my life. Wherever I turned, I saw death and injury, horrible injury—not actual death and injury, but death and injury to come. The frequency and intensity of my premonitions made each day a horror. I stood among my fellow soldiers and I knew which of them would not survive this war, which of them would come back disabled, crippled, or mangled. I knew how and when they would receive their wounds and I desperately wanted not to know. This knowledge made relationships impossible and it destroyed any chance I had for peace of mind.

Far from the repressive atmosphere of Van Buren now, I had an increasing number of other visions. For instance, I recall telling my commanding officer that there was going to be a big plane crash on the base very soon, in which lives would be lost. Not long ago, I described this incident at a lecture and a lady in the audience, who was at Fort Bragg at the time, told me she remembered the crash vividly.

Later, while on bivouac, I told the soldiers I was with that the war with Germany would be over by the time we returned. When we marched back to camp, the newspapers were using their biggest type faces to proclaim V-E Day.

My commanding officer heard about my prediction and called me into his office. "How did you know, Tanous? Or was it just a lucky guess?"

"A lucky guess? Maybe so," I told him. "But I'm always making lucky guesses like that. Maybe it isn't luck at all."

"Then what is it?"

I thought it was best not to go into detail. "I have something even more interesting to predict," I said. "Sometime in mid-August [1945] an extremely unusual bomb will explode in Japan and, as a result, the war will end there too."

I came out of the Army an adult. And when I went home, I found things had changed there, too. Far from discouraging her children's psychic experiences, my mother had begun to have some of her own. People were starting to come to her for readings. These proved unusually accurate and perceptive.

One day, not long after I got out of the service, I was sitting in the family living room when a woman visitor asked my mother for a reading. Mother took out the cards, as my father had done years earlier. She was about to start the reading when another thought occurred to her.

"No," she said, "I'm going to let my son do this reading." She handed me the cards. Now I'd had many psychic experiences in my life and I'd many times watched my father give readings. But I'd never done one of my own.

I told the woman to cut the deck into three parts and pick out several cards. To this day, I don't know why I did it this way. I do know that the cards had absolutely no significance. The message came to me when I took the woman's hand—it was a vision of her husband's death.

Reluctantly—I'd lost my youthful impetuosity—I told her what I saw: that within ten days, her husband would die. As I said these words, he wasn't even sick, so far as anyone knew. Ten days later, my prediction had been borne out, to my sorrow.

My mother never questioned me again, nor did she ever influence me to reject my psychic experiences. She realized that though I had grown up, my abilities had not left me. And now I was the man of the family, able to pick up where my father had left off.

Years later, I asked her why she'd had me do the reading. She said, "One night, while I was sleeping, I heard a choir of voices—angelic voices. I got up and checked the radio. It was off. I tiptoed into your room, but you were sound asleep. Yet the voices continued. In some way, I knew they were trying to tell me something about one of my children. You were the only one I was worried about, so I knew the message concerned you. I decided at that moment that you had to live your life as you would, that I could not interfere."

My mother's support hadn't ended the conflict between my religion and my psychic self, but it had added strength to my decision to do what I felt was right.

After this reading, I considered what I had done. I wasn't overjoyed by what I'd had to tell this woman, but I had done nothing against the dictates of my conscience. Still, one thing bothered me— the cards. Church canons specifically held that using cards to foretell the future was the devil's work. I knew this might disturb the people of Van Buren and it couldn't do our family any good.

The solution was simple enough. I abandoned the cards. They meant nothing to me anyhow. I'd used them only in imitation of my father. From that time on, I relied simply on hand contact between myself and my subject, psychometry. And my readings took on the form of conversations. People would tell me about their problems, their hopes and their fears, and I would tell them what came to me, relying on what I sensed by touch.

Death continued to loom large in my psychic sight. One day, a woman came to me and asked when her son would be released from the Army. "He's coming back very soon," I said, "but I want you to tell him not to cross railroad tracks by car. I see great danger to him in that situation." The boy arrived home shortly afterward, just as I had predicted. And three days after he came home, he was killed while driving over an unmarked railroad crossing in St. Leonard, New Brunswick, Canada, just across the river from Van Buren—also as I had predicted. How I knew this was going to happen, I don't know.

I'm glad to say that most of my visions were not this grim. I also could foresee when an old friend would unexpectedly drop in on the family, when someone would have a happy surprise—like a promotion or a bonus, when someone would get married (and often, to whom), that a previously childless couple would be blessed with children. My precognition included little things, such as knowing who would be calling when the phone rang, or where a lost object could be found, and big things, such as knowledge of whether a missing person was dead or merely lost, or who would be nominated and elected in political contests.

In those days, I didn't realize the importance of keeping precise records of predictions, so I cannot now list who was involved in what prediction, or when. What I've told you so far comes only from memory, and a rather hazy memory at that, since for some reason I am not often able to recall my psychic visions.

In later years, however, I kept exact records of time, place, date, person, and prediction. I also took care to obtain affidavits from the people involved and any witnesses. My files are bulging with such statements, and in later chapters I will quote from them extensively.

When I returned from the service, I went to work almost immediately to help my mother raise the rest of my brothers and see that they completed at least their high school educations.

I held down a number of jobs in this period, none of them very glamorous. I was still too unsettled to think in terms of a career. Besides, I still hoped to go to college someday, despite my poor high school grades and our shaky family finances.

One of my most interesting jobs was as a newspaper stringer for the *Aroostook Republican,* of Caribou, Maine. No sooner had I accepted the position when my psychic nature made itself felt. In the employment interview, my editor explained what sort of news he was looking for. "What you'd really like is a murder, right?" I asked.

"Well," he said, "I don't expect anything like that from a sleepy little town like Van Buren."

"You never can tell," I said. I had a premonition, but I didn't want to come right out and say it. Like every new employee, I was cautious.

Three days later, when I made my routine morning check with the local police department, I found out there'd been a strange death the night before. I called my editor. "Guess what?" I said. "There's been a murder in Van Buren." He dropped the phone in astonishment. Later, a verdict of suicide was rendered, but many people continued to wonder about the circumstances of the death.

Throughout the time I worked as a newspaper stringer, my psychic abilities stood me in good stead. I became known as a reporter with a real "nose for news." Several times I knew about events before they occurred and I always seemed to know where to go for more information about things that had already happened.

About the same time, I dabbled in song writing—even though I knew very little about music, having taken only a few piano lessons. I am convinced my psychic abilities helped me here, too.

I sent my first attempts at composing to a composer I admired greatly, W. C. Handy. He wrote back and told me that I had definite talent, that I should keep at it.

So I began composing songs. My first, a song called "Maytime," was eventually sold to Savoy Records. Though it was a pop song, Savoy decided to make it into a Western number and had it recorded by Lazy Bill Huggins and his group. It sold quite well. Then I wrote, "The Sands of Texas in My Boots," thinking that

Western music might be my forte. This, too, was recorded and sold well. So did another Western number I wrote, "I've Got the Blues."

When hymns came into vogue, I wrote one called "Let's Say a Rosary Each Day," which was also published, then recorded. I was delighted at how well it sold.

I wrote several other songs in addition to these, many of which were published. The royalties were modest by today's standards, even when taken in total, but they were welcome.

I never made a career of composing, but my interest in music has continued over the years. At one point, I did a number of popular song arrangements, several of which were picked up and used by some very famous singers.

In 1961, I wrote a three-and-a-half hour symphony called "America in Jazz." It was submitted to a French musical research group and performed at a music festival in France, where it won a Grand Prix. Later, selections from the symphony were played all over the world.

In 1963, I wrote "The Mass in Jazz," the first jazz mass ever written in Latin. This piece won a Musical Religious Award. The piece has had an enormous effect on the music used in Church Masses.

Just as I was making plans for college, war struck again—the Korean conflict. I was quickly recalled to service and sent to Fort Devens, Massachusetts. I spent two years in the U. S. Army Public Information Department. Actually, my assignment was much broader than public affairs, but I cannot describe it at this time, nor can I relate the details because of confidentiality.

This stint in the Army wasn't the torture that the last had been. My contact with combat troops was slight enough that I wasn't plagued by the overwhelming premonitions of death and injury that had clouded my days during my World War II hitch.

I continued to have psychic experiences, however. The one and only time I had to stand guard at Fort Devens, something odd happened to me. I was guarding some barracks when my commanding officer drove up in a jeep. "Hello, Tanous. Everything all right?" he asked.

"Things are okay now, but I have a feeling something is burning. I think there's going to be a fire or an explosion."

The officer gazed at me for a moment with a skeptical expression on his face, then shrugged and drove off. Before he was out of sight, there was a huge explosion about five hundred yards from where I was standing. The officer swerved around and drove back to me in a hurry. "How did you know?" he asked, flabbergasted.

"I don't know," I said. "I just had this feeling." And that was the truth.

While in the service this time, I met Eddie Fisher, the singer, and we became good friends. Through him, I met many other famous show business personalities. Before long, I found myself considering the idea of a show business career. Because of my voice and manner of speaking, many people had told me I might do well in radio.

When I got out of the Army in 1952, I enrolled at the Cambridge School of Radio and Television in Boston (now Grahm Junior College). As part of its curriculum, this school had an arrangement with WCOP for its students to take over certain programs so they would get live broadcasting experience.

One Saturday afternoon in mid-December, I was doing a Western music show when I came to a record of Hank Williams singing his "Cold, Cold Heart."

"Now here," I said over the air, "is *the late* Hank Williams, singing 'Cold, Cold Heart.'"

When I got off the air, the disc jockey who usually did the program came over to me, puzzled. "Do you know what you said?" he asked. "You called Hank Williams *the late* Hank Williams—and he isn't dead."

"I couldn't have done that," I said. "I know he's alive."

We checked with people in the studio and sure enough, I'd said, "the late." On January 1, 1953, less than two weeks later, Hank Williams was dead of a heart attack.

Was this simply a slip of the tongue, a coincidence? If it had happened to almost anyone else, they almost certainly would have dismissed it as nothing more than that. But I'd had too many similar experiences to think this one was just an accident of speech. I am convinced it was an instance of psychic foresight.

All during this time, I continued to give readings. On one occasion, I did one for Suzanne Zebeh, now Mrs. Ralph Azzie. A few years ago, she wrote me about what I'd said and how my predictions had been borne out:

"The first time I met you, in 1952, you told me I wouldn't marry before 1960 and I did not—until 1960. You told me there would be a sudden change in my work and you described to a 'T' the person responsible. You told me of a lengthy illness in the family—it turned out to my brother Philip. I saw you again in 1959, whereupon you told me that I could not and would never believe the wonderful things in store for me. Can you think of anything better than what transpired from 1960 on—a wonderful husband, four lovely children, a healthy, happy, loving home?"

It wasn't long before I realized I wasn't cut out to be a disc jockey. It gave me little opportunity to use the gift I'd been given. More and more, I felt called to religion. And I felt I needed an education to make the best use of my abilities.

Schooling—The Psychic Way

In the fall of 1953, nine years and two wars after I had graduated from high school, I entered Stonehill College, a Catholic-run school right outside of Brockton, Massachusetts. My intention was to become a priest.

If someone told me at the time that I would end up with a bachelor's degree, three master's degrees, finish my work on a Ph.D., and receive a doctorate of divinity, I would have doubted his sanity. Yet that's exactly what happened, and under the most astonishing circumstances.

My college career did not have a promising beginning. Possibly because of my weak high school background, I was in academic trouble from the start. I knew nothing about study techniques. During lectures, my mind drifted away easily. I failed several courses, though I struggled on.

On a couple of occasions my psychic nature helped me out. Once, while walking to an exam with my teacher and some fellow students, I predicted the questions we'd be asked. My predictions turned out exactly right. Another time while taking a test, I didn't understand a question. I asked the teacher to explain it and he opened his book, looking for a way to make it clearer. Somehow, I picked the explanation out of his mind, tuning in on what he was reading. "Thank you, Father," I said, before he could speak. I proceeded to answer the question properly, with no further explanation from him.

My psychic abilities also got me in trouble. In 1955, in my second year at Our Lady of Holy Cross Seminary at Stonehill College, one of my friends hurt his foot badly. He was put on crutches. One day, I saw him struggling up a long stairway. Suddenly, it came to me that I should go to him and tell him, "You are well, you can go up those stairs without crutches." I took the crutches from him and I said, "John, walk up those stairs. I know you can do it." And he did. Whether I had healed him or whether I somehow knew he had recovered from his accident I cannot say. But it happened. Soon, it was the talk of the school.

It wasn't long before the priests got a whiff of the incident. I was called on the carpet and thoroughly blasted. "It was just a feeling that I had to express," I said. "I have a lot of these feelings." In the end, I was left off with a warning and told I'd been "imprudent." But the atmosphere at the seminary had turned cold. And the conflict between my religion and my psychic nature had been revived.

After completing three years at the seminary, I was sent to the Holy Cross Novitiate in Bennington, Vermont, in August 1956, to see if I should continue in the religious life. My brothers David and Nolan came to visit me. As I shook hands with them, I had a premonition. I knew both of them were going to die before their time. The feeling about David was especially strong.

I told this to one of the priests, who pooh-poohed it. "Come on, Tanous," he said. "It's only your imagination." I tried to forget about it, but the feeling only got stronger.

In February 1957, David had an operation which revealed that he was filled with cancer, that he had less than six months to live. On September 11, 1957, I visited with him for the last time, at the hospital.

"I thought I died last night," he told me. "I saw my body as if I were standing on the other side of the room and looking at it. It was so beautiful that I didn't want to come back. I'm not afraid to die now." Today, I realize that he had had an out-of-body experience.

Before he died, David told Rev. Stanley Bowe, the Jesuit priest who was preparing him for death, that he would give a sign when he entered whatever it is we call heaven. He also said he would see that the Jesuits got a new residence, somehow.

On September 12, 1957, David died. He had been married a year and eleven days. On September 20, his wife, Esther, gave birth to a baby boy. While she was still in Mercy Hospital, Father Bowe rushed to her room and told Esther he believed David was in heaven.

"How can you know that?" she asked.

"You know how David loved St. Theresa and her roses?" Father Bowe asked. "Well, this morning, in spite of my flu, I went to say Mass. Suddenly, my nose was unblocked and for the first time in several days I could breathe. And you know what? The whole chapel was filled with the scent of roses. And there hadn't been flowers of any kind in the chapel. There's no doubt in my mind that it was David, fulfilling his promise."

Seven years later, almost exactly on the anniversary of David's death, an anonymous donor gave the Jesuits a new residence. Whether or not that, too, was David fulfilling his promise, I cannot say. But he had made exactly that pledge.

At the Holy Cross Novitiate, I was told by the provincial that it was decided by all parties, that the studies for the priesthood would be too difficult for me. They asked me to remain as a brother. I decided against it. I was convinced I would someday be ordained. I still am. But the time was not right.

In the fall of 1957, I entered Boston College to complete the three semesters of school I needed to get my degree. I promptly found myself in the deepest academic trouble of my life. Almost before I had begun, I was on the verge of flunking out of school altogether. I wasn't just having trouble in one course—I was having trouble in almost all of my courses.

One of my teachers laid it on the line. There was an exam coming up in my worst course—history, ironically. If I didn't score 100 on it, I could pack up my bags and go home. My college career would be over. Worst of all, it was going to be a short-answer exam, a combination of true-or-false and multiple-choice; I could usually handle essay tests, because I could always relive and visualize the events in question. But short-answer exams were my nemesis.

As it happened, I was then going to school with my youngest brother Tommy. I told him about the ultimatum. I was discouraged, ready to go home, and forget about both the test and college. "Take the test," he urged me. "After all, the GI bill is paying for it. And why don't you use your ESP on it? I'm sure it would help."

I really don't know why this hadn't occurred to me before. Possibly it was because I'd always been reluctant to use my gift for personal benefit. But Tommy's suggestion hit home. By this time, I'd heard that Edgar Cayce had learned the contents of a book merely by flipping through the pages, putting it under his pillow, and sleeping on it. So I did the same thing.

I took the exam the next day. Later, my teacher called me into his office. "You must have cheated, that's the only possible explanation."

"What do you mean?" I asked.

"You got your 100," he said. He still couldn't believe it.

From that moment on, I had no more troubles in school. Something had clicked in my mind. I flipped through my books, slept on them, and learned what I needed to know. After that, my grades were excellent—though I didn't always get 100 on my exams, of course.

I did particularly well in philosophy. My teacher had often witnessed me making psychic statements in class about philosophy and many other subjects and was impressed with me.

Maybe that's why I yielded to the extraordinary, almost absurd, psychic impulse that next struck me. It suggested that I should apply for graduate school at Boston College, that I should try to get a master's degree in philosophy. It further suggested that I apply for a scholarship.

Considering my scholastic record, this was a laughable idea, on the face of it. But I applied, as my psychic self had urged. I was accepted and I was awarded a full tuition scholarship.

The days that followed were filled with psychic experiences. I began to get a kind of following at Boston College, students who were interested in ESP and the paranormal.

One of these was a girl named Joanne Ireland Foley. One day, as a little test, she asked me to describe her sister's house in California. She'd never been there and she wanted to know what it looked like. While she and her friends listened, I described it in detail, via what I now know as an out-of-body experience. I closed my eyes and projected myself into that house. But there was one detail I couldn't get straight. There was a large chair in the living room that seemed to have no definite place. Joanne later talked to her mother, who'd seen the house, and confirmed my description in every detail. As for the chair, I was right there, too. It had no regular location. It was moved back and forth across the room for TV viewing.

Joanne told this story to one of her girl friends, a skeptic. One afternoon, while we were all sitting in the cafeteria, she challenged me to demonstrate my abilities.

"You have an unopened letter in your purse, an important one."

"No I don't," she said. "You're wrong."

"Take a look," I insisted. "I know I'm right."

She smiled as if to humor me. Then she frowned. "Wait a minute," she said. "You're right. I stuffed a letter into my purse when I was hurrying out of my house after breakfast. I forgot about it."

"Let me have the letter—but don't open it."

She opened her purse and handed me the letter, not nearly so skeptical now. I took it, held it for a moment, then returned it to her, still sealed.

"Now, I want you to open the letter. I'll read it aloud while you read it silently, sitting here, where I am, at the other end of the table."

She ripped open the envelope. As she read the letter to herself, I spoke its contents, word for word. This caused quite a commotion at the college. The people who had witnessed this were thoroughly frightened. I wasn't surprised when I was called in by one of the priests. I was getting used to that kind of treatment.

But, by now, I was convinced that my "decision in conscience" had been the right decision. The old guilts and conflicts seemed behind me. And it was from that position that I talked with the priest. He listened with respect. He admitted that very little was known about psychic phenomena. And he declined to make any judgment about my demonstration. "But, I'd appreciate it if you'd quiet down," he said. "It's not a good idea to frighten the students."

Of course, the students were no longer frightened. They were fascinated. I gave many readings and demonstrated my abilities in many ways. Joanne Ireland Foley, for instance, had many times told me she was sure she'd never be married. I reassured her, without much effect. Then one day, while both of us were in the language laboratory, a tall man neither of us had ever seen before walked in, looking for a teacher. Joanne told him where to find the teacher and he left. Then she turned and saw an odd expression on my face, as she described it.

"What's wrong, Alex?"

"That's the man you're going to marry."

"You're crazy!"

"No I'm not. You'll see."

Sure enough, they soon started dating. Eventually they married, just as I had predicted.

About this time, I got worrisome news from home. My mother, who had been sick for some time, had taken a turn for the worse. I met my brother Nolan in Portland. We got in the car and headed for home. Suddenly, a strange feeling came over me. "Slow down, Nolan. In fact, stop please." He asked why. "Because Mother has just died." I glanced into the night sky just in time to see a shooting star flash across the heavens. I glanced at my watch. It was eleven. Nolan and I finally arrived at home at five in the morning, only to find that my mother had died—at eleven the night before.

I believe I have heard from my mother many times since then. The most remarkable occasion came in 1964, when I was teaching at Manhattan College in New York. I became very ill then and I began passing blood. I flew to the Lahey Clinic in Boston. Doctors there told me I "had all the symptoms of cancer." They decided to do an exploratory.

But I wasn't ready for an exploratory, not then. That coming Monday, I had to give my students their final exam, then grade it. I promised the doctors I'd be back the following Friday. They reluctantly agreed. I gave the test, graded the papers, and told my students I was going into the hospital and I didn't know what might happen.

Wednesday night, I had a dream. My dead brothers, as well as my mother were all in this dream, with their backs to me. I thought I was being prepared to die, to join them. Strangely, my father wasn't there. I still don't know why.

The next day, Thursday, I went to confession. Thursday night, I had the dream once more. But my mother and brothers had now turned to face me. My mother was holding a single red rose. Like my brother David, she knew I always favored St. Theresa, and knew I loved the roses associated with the saint.

Suddenly, something told me I was cured, that there was nothing wrong with me any more. I called my girl friend and told her, then fell asleep. When I woke up, I knew I needed some sign to confirm my feeling.

My girl friend met me that morning and put me on the plane, certain she would never see me again. My family met me in Boston, afraid that yet another member of the family was about to pass on. I insisted that I was cured, but my family didn't believe me.

As I walked into my hospital room with the nurse, I saw a single fresh red rose in a vase on the dresser—and in the middle of February. "Where did that come from?" I asked the nurse.

She looked at it, unbelieving. "I could swear it wasn't here a moment ago," she said.

Later that day, the doctors examined me in preparation for the operation. They could find nothing wrong with me. Even the bleeding had stopped. What's the explanation? I have to admit, I don't know. But I believe that my mother somehow intervened and cured me.

I completed my master's work at Boston College in a single year, finishing in June 1960. A few days before I was to take my orals, my brother Nolan, the brother I'd had a premonition about back in August 1956, disappeared on a fishing trip, along with some companions. I couldn't concentrate on my tests and failed them. But a year later, I passed with flying colors and got my degree.

Counting my brother Nagle, who died early in 1958 of complications of rheumatic fever, I had lost three brothers, my mother and a nephew in a little more than two years. If Kahlil Gibran had been right about my powers, he had also been right about my sorrows.

After graduating from Boston College, I applied to Fordham University. I decided that I would aim for a doctorate in philosophy.

I was accepted at Fordham, but there was no scholarship involved. I told the head of the Philosophy Department, Father Summerville, S.J., that I would work and take weekend classes. It might take me a long time to get my degree that way, but I had no choice.

While I was telling this to Father Summerville, his office phone rang. It was the dean of men, Father Farricker, S.J. He told Father Summerville he needed a resident counselor. The position carried a full scholarship, room and board, medical expenses, phone—everything. Was it luck that I happened to be sitting in Father Summerville's office at that precise moment? I don't think so.

Father Summerville sent me to Father Farricker and the two of us hit it off as though we'd known each other all our lives. I got the job. Some might call this luck, but it was the kind of luck I'd had all my life, I believe—good fortune of the psychic sort.

While I was at Fordham, I served as a subject for some tests in connection with research Fordham was doing for the Navy. The Navy was trying to devise a night-landing guidance system for carriers, using special lights that created an illusory flight path. To the astonishment of the scientists who had designed the system, I could see right through the illusion, to the actual lights. It was another in the long line of strange happenings involving my eyes and light.

In 1964, I received my second master's degree, this one in theology, from Fordham University. The next year, I began teaching theology at Manhattan College in New York City. Then I shifted over to St. John's University in Brooklyn, where I taught theology through 1967.

It was during this period that I was an observer at the Ecumenical Council. I visited the council in 1962, 1963, and 1964. There, because of my interest in theology, I was given special permission to listen to the council's deliberations.

Thus, I was privileged to hear the discussions that led to the establishment of the "Doctrine of Conscience," the rule that allows Catholics to make up their own minds on moral issues, so long as there is no dogma covering the subject.

The Doctrine of Conscience allowed me, at last, to make peace with myself, to resolve the internal conflicts between my psychic nature and my religious beliefs. It freed me to embrace the psychic world and permitted me to stay true to my faith.

The years of conflict had come to an end, though there would be new conflicts in the future.

The doctorate work at Fordham was not the end of my education. Later, in 1965, I received my doctorate of divinity at the College of Divine Metaphysics (The Divinity College of Indiana),

Indianapolis, Indiana. And in June 1973, I was awarded my master's degree in counseling and guidance from the University of Maine, where I got straight A's.

About that time, I was also accredited as a school psychologist. In addition, I became a marriage counselor. In the course of all this education, I picked up a working knowledge of nine languages.

Incidentally, not once in all these years did I cram or study in the usual sense. I learned the psychic way, flipping through the pages of my books, then sleeping on them.

The extent of my education makes me highly unusual among psychics, by the way, as almost all of them are unlettered or have limited educations, so far as I know.

The Teaching Years

For about ten years (with brief interruptions) teaching was my profession. Today, however, I look upon that time as a period of preparation, a period of trial. When I had finally passed through it, I was ready to fully assume the psychic mantle.

The teaching years were filled with a growing sense of comfort with and confidence in my psychic powers. I found that I could not only perform psychic feats myself, I could show others how to tap their psychic abilities.

At St. John's University, for example, after a long classroom discussion on Christ and the paranormal, I decided to demonstrate the existence of psychic phenomena by using the students themselves. I asked several students to leave the room—one at a time—while others inside the room drew pictures on pieces of paper and sealed them in envelopes. Then, the student outside the room was asked to come in and draw on the blackboard whatever picture he'd picked up mentally while standing outside. A number did remarkably well. One in particular, who'd pooh-poohed the idea of telepathy, showed exceptional abilities. His performance so upset him that I had to spend quite a while with him after class reassuring him.

On other occasions at St. John's, I sealed picture postcards in envelopes and passed them around. I then asked the students to describe what they thought was in the envelopes. The results were significant enough to show that something had happened—though just what was not clear. Either I was transmitting the picture to the students telepathically or they were using abilities of their own. There was no doubt, however, that something paranormal had occurred.

For the first time in my life, I also began to make predictions in public, to groups of people. It was at this time I said Robert Kennedy would be President—if he didn't get shot. I also predicted that Richard Nixon would be nominated for the presidency, though he hadn't yet announced his candidacy. I foretold the death of the U.S. astronauts in a non-space accident and my prediction was borne out. I predicted that a vote to admit Red China to the United Nations would fail, which it did. I said that a petition to remove Governor Ronald Reagan of California would be circulated, and it was. I said a Negro named Marshall would be appointed to the Supreme Court long before anyone had mentioned Thurgood Marshall for the post.

It was now that I began to lecture, both on psychic phenomena and religion. I talked about the paranormal events described in the Bible and spoke of Christ as the greatest psychic of all time. I talked also of the Church's coming troubles and of the difficulties parochial schools would face. At the time, no one believed me, but everything I said has come to pass.

All during this time—throughout my college and teaching years —I also led a very active social life. Outside of the usual flirtations and brief relationships, I was close to marriage on four separate occasions. Each time, I asked my psychic self whether or not I should go ahead. On every occasion but one, the answer was "No."

The first time, when I decided against marriage, the woman in question entered a convent. The second time, my psychic voice counseled delay. During the delay, I was separated from the woman for a long time, during which what had been romantic love turned into the love friends share.

The third time, my psychic voice said, "Yes"—but it was a sarcastic yes, as if the real meaning was, "Yes, go ahead and marry her, but it won't do you any good." Before I had a chance to act on what my psychic voice had told me, she was dead.

The fourth time (and, to date, the last time), my psychic voice reminded me of my earlier conviction that I would someday be ordained as a priest, something marriage would have made impossible, of course. Once again, I chose not to marry.

For a time, this decision seemed a remarkable foreshadowing of future events. In 1967, soon after deciding against marriage, while I was still teaching at St. John's, I met Bishop Francis Zayek, now Bishop of St. Maron Diocese, Detroit, and head of the Maronite People in America at Our Lady of Lebanon Church in Brooklyn, through the pastor, Rt. Rev. Msgr. Mansour Stephen, C.B. (Chor Bishop). When Bishop Zayek and I shook hands, he gazed at me with an odd expression.

"Dr. Tanous," he said, "it is my belief that God has called you to become a priest."

Because of my similar conviction, reinforced by the decision against marriage I had made so recently, Bishop Zayek's words had special power for me. I felt as though I had reached another crossroads in my life. Soon after, I resigned from St. John's and enrolled at Catholic University in Washington, D.C., to learn canon law, study the Arabic Mass, and acquire other knowledge needed to become a priest.

If I had been ordained on schedule, it would have been the first time in America that a man had been ordained in the Maronite Rite without having to go through many years of study at a seminary. That special privilege was granted me because of Bishop Zayek's conviction that I was predestined for the priesthood.

But it was not to be, at least not then.

When I left for Washington, I was perfectly content with the idea that I was going to become a priest. I took up residence at the nearby Maronite seminary and began my studies.

Then an inexplicable event occurred which had profound consequences for me. One evening, I went with my superior to a nondenominational dinner. After the dinner, the guest speaker was David Duplessy, who spoke in the pentecostal manner.

Addressing a rather large audience, Duplessy began to speak of the gifts of the Holy Spirit. He was talking about the Ecumenical Council (1962–65) and the changes that had come out of it. But the way he spoke, it sounded like faddish, fanatic religiosity.

I had been to the Ecumenical Council, one of the few laymen to attend, and I felt he wasn't giving the correct impression. For me, the most important change to come from the Ecumenical Council was the Doctrine of Conscience, which allowed me to abide by my own beliefs, even if the Church disagreed with these beliefs. This new doctrine finally laid to rest the conflict between my psychic self and my religion.

But Duplessy spoke of how the Spirit was at work, how the people would be given the gifts of prophecy, the gifts of healing, etc., and how a new generation of human beings—different human beings—would build a new kind of world.

I thought this was all silly nonsense. But the rest of the audience seemed in awe, as if they hoped they would be the recipients of these gifts. I was the mocker. I was the one who was nudging my superior, Msgr. Elias El Hayek, and saying, "Come on now, this is a lot of ridiculous nonsense."

Suddenly, with no warning whatever, something happened to me.

I felt filled with a kind of light. I screamed! And I'm not the sort to scream. I let out an AMEN! that shook the rafters. In the midst of my amused skepticism, I had become changed—energized.

Something within me said, "You must leave the seminary and go into the world. I will guide you in your true work, your psychic work." I did not reveal this vision to my colleagues, but soon after I left Catholic University, taking a leave of absence.

Even today, I cannot explain what happened to me in Washington, D.C. I take it as a sign, the first of two remarkable omens that led me to my present calling, that of practitioner of the psychic arts and sciences.

In September 1968, I took up a new job as teacher of marriage and theology courses at St. Anselm's, a Catholic college in Manchester, New Hampshire. Today, I realize that what happened at St. Anselm's was part of my period of trial. At the time, it seemed like an unmitigated disaster.

I'd been at St. Anselm's for less than two months when the Manchester *Union Leader*—the paper published by William Loeb—contacted me through the school's public relations office. Evidently, someone at the paper had heard of my predictions and my psychic experiences and wanted to find out if my abilities were genuine.

Eventually, I was interviewed by one of the paper's top reporters, Carol Morrisey. The result was a long story published in the *Union Leader* November 2, 1968. The title: *He Is Able to Predict the Future*. Among other things, it said:

"Many who scoff at ouija boards, divining rods, crystal balls and extrasensory perception will probably doubt the ability of Alexander Tanous to 'predict the future'—that is, until they meet him. . . .

"He has foretold events of national and international significance, as well as situations and occurrences meaningful to friends, relatives and acquaintances. His gift of perception is widely recognized. . . ."

The newspaper story proved to be very controversial at St. Anselm's. Some of the faculty and the administration, I believe, did not approve of what had been said about me and they weren't happy that I'd been identified as assistant professor at their school. It didn't matter that I'd never said a word about psychic phenomena in any of my classes. These feelings were communicated to me very clearly.

Now that I'd made my personal peace with my religion and my psychic abilities, I felt that neither St. Anselm's nor the Church was qualified to judge my work in the paranormal. The Church knew little about such things. And as for St. Anselm's, what I did in my private life, so long as it was decent and honorable, quite simply was none of their affair.

While the school was evidently displeased by the publicity, the newspaper's readers were fascinated. They wanted more. In December, the *Union Leader* came to me and asked me for a list of predictions about what would happen in 1969. I gave them one.

Among other things, I predicted that Eugene McCarthy would have marital troubles (he was divorced that year, though there'd been no hint of trouble when I made my forecast); that De Gaulle's health would fail (he died); that California would rule out the dealth penalty (it did); that Eisenhower would die that year of a heart attack (he did); that Judy Garland would make headline news (she did—she died); that after four miscarriages, Sophia Loren would give birth to a healthy baby boy (she did); that more nuns, brothers, and priests would leave the Church than ever before (they did); and that a great scandal would come out of the American government. (I was a bit premature here.)

The articles were a smashing success everywhere except at St. Anselm's. There, it brought me more criticism.

Others felt differently. When in the nearby village of Allenstown, eleven-year-old Debbie Horn disappeared, I was called in to help. I told her parents she was alive and near a big city not far away. I told them what to do to get her back. The Manchester *Union Leader* printed the story with my instructions. One result was a hoax—a man asking for money who had nothing to do with the kidnaping. When the hoax story appeared in the papers, I felt the kidnapers were frightened. As a result, I believe, the girl was killed.

During the course of the search, I was several times asked by the press about the girl's fate and I said, "No comment." But I knew the girl was dead. Since then, I never speak about such cases to the papers until they've been closed or otherwise resolved.

The Debbie Horn case and the attendant publicity brought matters to a head at St. Anselm's. In early February I was notified that my teaching contract would not be renewed for another year. They obviously wanted no part of a man who had good reason to believe he could perform psychic feats, who could see into the future.

Approximately eleven hundred of the fourteen hundred students at St. Anselm's signed a petition demanding to know why I had been terminated, but the school gave them no satisfaction. College officials refused to discuss the subject with the *Union Leader*, calling it a "private matter."

But it had some time ago ceased to be a private matter. The controversy over my St. Anselm's troubles (and later termination) had already spread to the pages of *Church World*, the Catholic newspaper. There, I was both attacked and defended for my forecasts and other psychic experiences. Some of my critics saw a clash between my role as a Catholic theologian and my adventures in the paranormal.

But in the January 17 issue of *Church World*, the Reverend Clement D. Thibodeau said that the Church had previously failed "to distinguish between the natural phenomena and the occult, since they often confused the two themselves. Today, there are serious efforts being made . . . to establish the . . . factual basis for the many astounding but undeniable phenomena once condemned as Black Magic. ESP is a fact."

Despite the controversy and the protests, when the school year came to an end in June 1969, I was out of a job. I left St. Anselm's and went home (now East Millinocket, Maine) with a great faith that something would lead me in the right direction. Regardless of what had happened to me, I was at peace with myself.

Looking back on the incident today, I almost feel as though it was foreordained. If I had continued at St. Anselm's, I might still be a teacher today, content with my lot. As it was, my termination there was catalytic, leading me to my calling more quickly than any other course of events I can imagine.

While at St. Anselm's, I had given lectures several times in various cities and towns throughout New England, usually for schools for the blind or similar institutions. These were fund-raising lectures, usually given to packed houses. I received nothing more than my expenses and the pleasure I received from helping people. I especially enjoyed the period after the lectures, when the crowd would hold me there for hours, asking questions, talking about personal problems.

Through these lectures, I came to the attention of WGAN, a Portland, Maine, radio station. It was instituting a call-in talk show called "Maine Line." The program's host, Craig Worthing, wanted me as a guest.

I agreed, perhaps too hastily. When I thought about it, I got worried. I knew people would be calling in, asking questions, expecting answers. In the past, I'd been able to do this only when holding the questioner's hand. Now I would have to respond to a disembodied voice, coming in over the phone. Could I do it?

The night before the show, I realized I didn't have to depend on psychometry—touching—to provide the answers that would be expected. I had another technique at my command: out-of-body travel (also known as astral-projection). When asked a question, I could instantly leave my body, travel to any point in space or time —past, present, or future—and return with the answer.

Recently, I had done this several times, not to mention even stranger, even more inexplicable feats. But the details of these belong in a later chapter.

My appearance on "Maine Line" was an unprecedented success. I proved to skeptics and believers alike that a psychic could give readings over the radio. The most spectacular example occurred on June 27, 1969. Mrs. Shirley Davis called in and asked me if I could locate a member of the family who was missing. She gave me no further information.

I sat back in my chair and, with the little information I had, tried to project myself to wherever this missing relative was. Disordered words came out of my mouth: "Texas, male, brother—he is not in Texas now, but in Maine. He usually comes by plane, but this time he did not come that way. I see cement and bars, place of confinement, a broken arm, mental stress, business is suffering badly, he is greatly depressed, physical condition has changed drastically, very confused, extensive use of alcohol, involved with other women, he had injuries to his back and legs from World War II, wears a brace for his back, he will be dead in three weeks, will fall slumped forward."

Even as I said this, I couldn't believe what I was doing. Among other things, I was predicting the death of a person I'd never seen, someone whose name I didn't even know. Yet every word of what I said proved true.

The woman was talking about her brother from Texas. Later, he was located in Maine. He usually flew there from Texas. This time, he drove. I'd said I'd seen cement and bars—his ex-wife had sent him to jail (where he'd fallen on the cement floor and broken his arm).

He was under great mental stress, as I'd said. His business was suffering badly, in fact, he'd recently had a bankruptcy. He wore a back brace because of injuries received during World War II, as I'd said. He drank heavily, he had been involved with women other than his wife, his physical condition had seriously deteriorated in recent months and his mental condition was poor. He was depressed and confused. I said on June 27 that he would be dead in three weeks and would fall slumped forward. On July 22, he shot himself. And fell forward. In this case, my predictions and their corroboration were heard by thousands of people in the WGAN area.

I was on "Maine Line" many other times that summer and since and I made hundreds upon hundreds of predictions, both personal and public. Later that year, for example, on October 3, 1969, when "Maine Line" was staged in an auditorium for a charitable benefit, I said, "The space program faces a setback in 1970. Apollo 13 will never make it to the moon. There will be an explosion. I feel the capsule will hit a magnetic field which NASA is not aware of. But the astronauts will return safely."

Some nine thousand people inside the auditorium heard this prediction, as did another three thousand people outside, listening to loudspeakers. At the same time, by the way, I predicted the date of the year's first snowstorm in the area, December 13. Both predictions went out over the UPI wire, nationwide.

The *National Enquirer* picked up my Apollo 13 prediction and printed it in its January 18, 1970, issue, and over the radio, I repeated what I had said about Apollo 13 just before it blasted off, on April 11.

We all know now that there *was* an explosion on board Apollo 13 while it was bound for the moon. We also know the crew returned safely, just as I had predicted. As for the magnetic field I mentioned —well, I'll have more to say about that later on.

Incidentally, the first snowstorm of the season in the Portland area took place on schedule—December 13.

Every time I was a guest on the "Maine Line" show, the WGAN phone system jammed up so badly no one could get through. Thousands of people were calling to ask me questions. In fact, the phone response to the program was so overwhelming that it overloaded Portland's entire telephone network. In certain areas of the city, it didn't matter who called whom—the line was busy.

WGAN bowed to the inevitable and gave me my own radio show, a one-hour program from six to seven every Saturday night. It ran for thirty weeks. On this show, I not only took calls from local residents, but I also talked long distance to many other famous American psychics—Jeane Dixon, Mrs. and Mrs. Ambrose Worrall, and David Bubar, among others. In addition, I interviewed others who'd reported strange experiences—people who'd had ghosts in their houses, people who'd seen flying saucers, people who'd had dreams or premonitions come to pass.

At the same time, I found myself a lecturer much in demand. When I wasn't on the radio, I was speaking to one group or another about the paranormal. And when I wasn't lecturing, I was giving personal readings. When I wasn't giving personal readings, I was trying to answer a few of the thousands of letters that to the astonishment and dismay of the post office were flooding my mailbox.

It had been less than a year since I left Washington, D.C., after my experience at their pentecostal meeting and come first to Manchester, New Hampshire—to St. Anselm's—and then back to Maine. Looking back on it, it seems that every step I took advanced me toward fame, though I was unaware of this at the time. It was as though my life were being manipulated somehow, by some force.

While I was happy to share my gift with others, either on the radio or by giving lectures, or responding to letters, or giving personal readings, I never sought fame. In fact, I began to have grave doubts about playing the role "circumstance" was laying out for me.

I was now devoting every waking minute to matters psychic or paranormal and if I'd had more time, I would have been forced to spend it the same way. Suddenly, I had gone from a period when the interest in my psychic abilities was mild at best (and often negative) to a time when people couldn't hear enough of what I had to say about all things psychic.

I'd never seen myself as a public figure, who would have to meet the demands of the public. In this respect, I was an innocent. But it didn't take me long to realize that my personal life was being rapidly eroded. Before long, I found that I had no personal life whatever. I couldn't go to a party and be just another guest. As soon as people found out my name, I was the center of attention. I couldn't date without giving readings for everyone in the girl's family, not to mention her friends and neighbors. I was stopped while walking down the street. My own family was beseiged by requests for my time.

Further, I knew that people believed in me and followed me—even when I was wrong. (And I am wrong sometimes, for reasons I'll get into later.) People were looking at me as if I were a god—or a devil. I remember once giving someone an apple and someone else saying—and not really in jest—"Don't eat that apple, it may be cursed." Another time, a person came to me and asked for my protection against evil spirits. And there were many similar incidents.

People either saw me as an angel, a saint, a miracle man or a kind of holy man, or as a demon, an evil spirit, a trafficker with the devil. I was both feared and worshiped.

This made me most uncomfortable. I know I am neither god nor devil. I am a person, with human frailties and human virtues. I wanted to be accepted as that and nothing more or less.

Because so many listened to and believed what I said, I felt an enormous responsibility. I felt it was my duty to find solutions to the thousands of problems people brought to me. I was convinced this was the way to use my gift. At the same time, I was not sure I was worthy. I was not sure I could meet the responsibility that had been thrust on me.

The greater my fame, the more intensely I questioned myself. To what limit must I go to serve others? How completely did I have to surrender my everyday life to my psychic nature? Was there room, between those who viewed me as doing the work of the devil and those who thought of me as godly, for a human being named Alex Tanous? Was I really worthy of my gift, despite my human imperfections?

As my fame—and the demands on my time—grew, so did my self-doubt. I was now accomplishing greater psychic feats than ever before, and with more frequency and consistency. Still, I did not know if I should take the ultimate step and become, in essence, a priest of psychic phenomena, who lived an austere, priestly life entirely devoted to his calling.

If I accepted this ordination of sorts, it meant taking on an enormous responsibility to those who came to me. And it meant the sacrifice of my personal life. But if I abandoned what was obviously my calling, it meant the denial of what I knew I was, and the renewal of profound internal conflicts, the same kind of conflicts that in my high school days had driven me to the brink of mental collapse.

These feelings slowly coalesced during the balance of 1969 and throughout 1970. At the same time, I continued my radio programs, my lectures and my readings, actually intensifying my schedule.

Meanwhile, I joined the faculty of Cheverus High School,

Portland, Maine, in fall 1970, where I taught French, psychology, and theology. And my psychic experiences continued. Earlier that year, I'd shaken hands with Bruce Campbell, a Cheverus teacher, and told him that his wife would become pregnant. I told him he would have a daughter.

"How do you know she'll become pregnant?" he asked.

I shrugged. "I don't know how I know—but I do."

"We already have four boys," he told me. "I've been wishing with all my might for a girl. So has my wife."

Later, Mr. Campbell's wife gave birth to a boy. I'd been half wrong, anyhow. They'd been hoping so hard for a girl that I tuned in on this wishful thinking rather than the actual future, when I made my prediction. At least, that's my theory.

For some, my work remained controversial. On one occasion, a priest refused to allow me to appear at a scheduled lecture at his church, even though my topic was to be theology, not ESP. More letters were printed in *Church World*, attacking me and defending me. One priest denounced me by name from his pulpit. On the next Sunday, I went to his church and, in front of the entire congregation, went to him for communion. He couldn't refuse.

And my popularity grew. I was invited to speak to various groups and organizations and fund-raising affairs and I attracted thousands of people at each speaking engagement.

When I started teaching at Cheverus, I gave up my own hour-long weekly radio show at WGAN, but continued to be practically a regular on "Maine Line," a talk show at the same station. Moreover, I was struggling to answer as many as I could of the nearly fifty thousand letters that had come to my apartment since I'd left St. Anselm's. My evenings and weekends were almost entirely devoted to personal readings.

It was all too much for me. Either I devoted myself entirely to my psychic life (except for teaching, by which I supported myself) or I changed gears and became a private person again. I couldn't continue to keep a foot in both worlds.

I was walking in a driving snowstorm in January 1971, when the issue came to a head. For days, I'd been engaged in mental argument with myself. I had been struggling over which path to take. If it were wrong to pursue my psychic life, I wanted God to take this ability from me. If not, I wanted some sign, some kind of omen that would help me decide which way to go. I was in anguish.

Striding through the snow, huddled up in my coat, head down, I silently asked God a question. "God, am I doing wrong or right? I've got to know." And in my mind, I suddenly heard a voice.

"Well, how can I prove to you that you're going in the right direction?"

In my normal mind, I never would have asked for what I did. "I want a miracle," I said. It was a crazy thing to ask for, but such was my mental state.

"What kind of miracle do you want?" said the voice in my mind.

And I said, "I want lightning to strike."

Snowstorms are rarely accompanied by lightning, especially cold snowstorms, such as this one. Up until that moment, there'd been no sign of electrical discharge. Yet at the moment I mentally pronounced the word "lightning" to myself, a broad bolt of lightning flashed across the sky. Afterward, there were no others.

"Thank you, God. I will never question you again." I knew I'd been given a sign that I was on the right path. I had wanted reassurance that my gift was God-given, that it had a purpose, that it was meaningful. I wanted to be told that this wasn't just a game in which I tried to prove my talents to a newspaper reporter, but that my gifts had some sort of larger meaning.

That day, I was given the answer I had sought. And from that moment on, I've simply done my best to meet my obligations as I see them, confident that I'll be given guidance if need be.

I did require that guidance on one occasion. In the middle of December 1971, I took ill. For a week, I had a temperature of up to 105°. Then I had an operation, during which a badly infected testicle was removed. Back in my room after the operation, when I had come out of the anesthesia, I wondered if my gift had survived. I thought, if my ability was centered in my brain, a result of some unusual structure there, it might have been burned out by my high fever. Well, I told myself, if that happened, I'd just start living a normal life.

No sooner had I thought these thoughts than the nurse who'd been in the recovery room with me came in and told me that I'd made a prediction while still partially anesthetized. Two days later, that prediction came true. The following is taken from a letter written to me by Mrs. Irene Myrick, recovery room technician at Mercy Hospital, Portland, Maine, on December 29, 1971:

"I first met Dr. Alex Tanous on December 16, 1971, following surgery. As a recovery room technician, my duty is to arouse the patient and keep him awake while talking to him. Dr. Tanous, still under the anesthetic given him, and I had the following conversation.

"I told him I had two boys, one in Vietnam, which is enough to cause any mother to worry. Dr. Tanous remarked that I had no need to worry about him. . . . He was all right and would soon be home. 'It will be a big surprise for all.' We—my husband and I—were previously informed that my son's camp would be closing sometime in March or May of '72, so naturally, my mind related to that as being the answer to it all. . . . On Sunday, December 19, the phone rang at 5:30 A.M. It was a call from my son. He had just arrived from Vietnam and was in Seattle, Washington, on his way home."

After two years at Cheverus, I joined the staff of another small high school, Thornton Academy, in Saco, Maine. There, I taught the first high school course in ESP ever given for credit. It was an elective and an exceptionally popular one.

"When Thornton Academy put an ESP course among its electives for fall, word about the class went through the school like wildfire," reported the Portland *Telegram* on December 24, 1972. "Registration had to close with 180 students in six divisions, not because all the interested students had been accommodated, but because 'there was just no time slot where we could schedule another section,' according to Paul Staples, head of the Thornton English department."

Since then, dozens of high schools and scores of colleges have begun offering similar courses covering many aspects of extrasensory perception, psychic phenomena, paranormal experiences, the mystic, and the occult, etc.

I left Thornton Academy at the end of the school year to devote myself entirely to the world of the paranormal. Since then, I have appeared on many radio and television programs, been the subject of countless newspaper and magazine articles, delivered I don't know how many lectures, spent many weeks in the laboratory at the American Society for Psychical Research in New York, and done my best to answer the continuing flow of mail. In the last four years, according to the U. S. Mail Service, I have received over a hundred and seventy thousand letters.

Over the years—and especially since I saw that lightning bolt—I have had an extraordinary variety of psychic experiences, some far more spectacular than any I've described up to now.

I've done literally thousands of personal readings about subjects significant and trivial with remarkable accuracy. I've diagnosed illness. More important, I've been able to heal many victims of disease or accident after conventional medical treatment has failed.

I've worked closely with the police in many different types of criminal cases and the information I've been able to provide from my psychic sources has often been instrumental in bringing these cases to a satisfactory conclusion.

I've had a large number of very odd experiences with machines—particularly cameras, tape recorders, and watches. Whatever energy source I have tapped seems to throw them out of whack. On other occasions, I've been the subject of some inexplicable psychic photography, in which everything in the picture appears normal except me. I'm invisible. I know that sounds unbelievable. I could hardly believe it myself, when I saw the photographs. But it's true.

I've had some even more incredible experiences with light. In these, I've been able to project balls of light into my hands or into the room, in otherwise absolute darkness. Other times, I've been able to project pictures and streaks of light on walls. I do not make such claims lightly. I know how unbelievable they are. But I have both witnesses and Polaroid photographs to back me up.

Under controlled laboratory experiences, with scientific instruments recording everything, I have left my body, identified objects in a distant room, then rejoined myself. I've also made remarkable scores on carefully administered ESP tests.

I've predicted many events of national and international significance and seen my predictions come true. I've made contact with ghosts and spirits, and convinced them to peacefully leave "haunted" houses. I've had weird experiences that lead me to believe there may be people on this planet who did not originate here. I've had visions about the destiny of mankind, about warnings from God and possible holocausts.

In the chapters that follow, I intend to describe and document all of these experiences in detail. I also intend to explain them, as best I can, and to show the "ordinary" person can do what I have done.

Predictions
About Public Persons
and Public Events

It was during my high school days, when I predicted the date of America's entry into World War II, that I first realized I could apply my psychic gifts to world events and public figures, as well as to private persons who asked me specific questions about their own lives.

That World War II prediction was followed up, in my early years, with predictions about the date of V-E Day, and the character and the date and place of the atomic bomb's first use.

In my college years, I continued to make predictions about important national and international events and persons. For example, when I entered Boston College in the fall of 1957, I predicted that John F. Kennedy would be the next President of the United States. This was at least a year before there was any serious speculation he would try for the post and eighteen months before he began to campaign.

For some reason, I did not foresee John Kennedy's assassination. However, I did see both trouble and opportunity ahead for Robert Kennedy. I said, "Robert Kennedy will be elected President—if he doesn't get shot first." Of course, many people were saying that, especially in the latter years of Johnson's administration. But I said it shortly after his older brother was assassinated. And I must stress that this statement came from psychic sources, not from political knowledge, logic, or simply good guessing.

Since that time, I have made frequent predictions about state, national, and even international politics, local and international economic conditions, diplomatic negotiations, matters of importance to the Church, even the outcome of sports events. I've made these predictions at lectures, on radio and television broadcasts and, beginning in 1969, I've had a list of NEW YEAR'S PREDICTIONS published in the newspapers every year.

Not all of my predictions have proved correct. And this is also true of my private readings. I have been wrong—sometimes ludicrously wrong—about 15 per cent of the time. I have some pretty good ideas why this is so and I intend to go into that subject when I talk about the explanation for my psychic abilities in a later chapter.

In public forums or in print, I predicted that Lyndon Johnson would not run again for the presidency—well in advance of his surprise speech to that effect. I also predicted that Richard Nixon would run and that he would win the Republican nomination. This was long before he announced his candidacy.

After Nixon was elected to his first term, I predicted American forces in Vietnam would undertake a major mission in Cambodia and this would quiet the war—for a while. I predicted Nixon's first two choices to fill the vacancy in the Supreme Court would be rejected by the Senate but that the third would be approved.

About this time, I also predicted the demise of America's military draft, many months before the idea was publicly discussed. I predicted that Juan Peron would return to power in South America —once more, well before he announced his intention to try. And, as I have said, I predicted the fate of Apollo 13, the only U.S. manned mission to run into serious trouble in space.

While Edmund Muskie was still the heavy favorite for Democratic nomination for President in the 1972 election, I predicted that George McGovern would win that honor. At the same time, I predicted that Nixon would swamp McGovern in the election itself. To be sure, many political commentators were saying the same thing, but I am sure their information came from conventional political intelligence. I received mine through psychic images or mental thoughts. Actually, I know very little about national politics.

Since I live so close to the Canadian border, I am often asked about Canadian Prime Minister Pierre Trudeau. In an interview by

E. Demerchant for *The Telegraph Journal*, I predicted exactly when the Prime Minister would marry. It came as a surprise to Canadians when it happened. There was no indication that this event was to take place. Then I correctly predicted the birth date of his second child.

On a Maine TV show, I predicted that there would be an assassination attempt on Pope Paul in Manila. This raised quite a furor, as he hadn't announced any trip at that time. But before long, the news of such a trip was released. And while he was in Manila, there was an attempt on the Pope's life.

On Craig Worthing's talk show in Miami (on station WINZ), on February 19, 1974, I predicted there would be an explosion in spring, in midtown Manhattan. Exactly such an explosion occurred. And, coincidentally, I trust, I was in New York at the time. At the same time, I also predicted that John Mitchell and Maurice Stans would be acquitted of charges against them in the Vesco case. This time, popular opinion disagreed vehemently. But my prediction proved true.

People frequently ask me about the Kennedys because I have made many predictions about them which have come true. I've had many premonitions about all of the Kennedy brothers. For instance, while speaking at a high school in Manchester, New Hampshire, in March 1969, I predicted that Ted would be involved in an accident, but not hurt. This was four months before the Chappaquiddick incident.

Later, after Chappaquiddick, I was questioned in detail about that accident. I made an attempt to relive it, as I had relived history in my school days. Over WABI, Channel 5, a television channel in Bangor, Maine, I told the truth as I saw it:

The Chappaquiddick incident was not an accident, but an assassination attempt. The car had been tampered with. And as I relived it, Ted Kennedy—luckily—was not in the car when the mishap occurred. He'd loaned it to Mary Jo Kopechne after she dropped him off. She went back to the party, then left, in the car, alone. The steering failed as she was going over the bridge. When the car and the girl failed to show up, Kennedy went looking for them. Eventually, he did dive down to the car, in a vain attempt to rescue Miss Kopechne, exactly as he said later.

Since I first told the story of what I had relived, I've found some support for my version of the event. The diver who went down to retrieve Miss Kopechne's body shortly after the accident found the car doors locked. In fact, he had to smash the windows to gain entry. For some reason, though this was reported in the press, no one paid much attention to it. Yet how could Ted Kennedy have left the car and locked the doors behind him?

Months later, I had occasion to talk to a man and his wife who went to Chappaquiddick after the mishap and knew something about what had happened there. They also believed that Ted Kennedy had not been in the car at the time of the accident.

It is my belief that the car had been tampered with. Why didn't Kennedy make this information public? My conviction is that he kept quiet because he feared what would happen to the country, that he was worried that many would be convinced there was a conspiracy against certain political views.

I have no further information on this subject, but my premonition is on file with the American Society for Psychical Research and at the Central Premonition Bureau, as are the details of many of my other predictions.

Whenever I appear on radio or TV, people call in to ask how their favorite sports team will do. I don't follow sports very closely, but I'm always happy to repeat what my psychic sense tells me.

On one such occasion, Bob Ridge of Portland, Maine, asked me how the National League East baseball race would turn out. Let me quote his recollection of what I said:

"On August 22, 1969, when the Chicago Cubs had a twelve and a half game lead in the National League East, Dr. Tanous told me that the New York Mets would come on to be the ultimate winner. And they did! Everyone was surprised. Bob Ridge, Portland, Maine."

Later, I was even more specific. But let Craig Worthing, host of the "Maine Line" show on WGAN, describe the details:

"Back in October 1969, Dr. Tanous and I did a show from Portland City Hall. We had 2,338 people inside and another 500 or 600 people outside, trying to get in.

"Alex came out, chatting about the World Series. Now earlier in the year, he'd picked the Mets to win. In those days, people didn't even know who the Mets were—it wasn't simply that they weren't favored to win. I said then, 'You're crazy, Alex.'

"We did our show just prior to the World Series. We knew it was going to be Baltimore vs. the New York Mets. I asked Alex, 'Who's going to win it?'

"And he said, 'I see the New York Mets in five games.'

"Now Alex doesn't know anything about the World Series. He knows nothing about baseball. If anyone saw the Mets winning that series—and few people did—they sure didn't see them winning in four out of the first five games. But that's exactly what they did."

Coincidence? Luck? Possibly. But can anyone call it mere luck when a man who knows nothing about horse racing predicts an unlikely winner in a major race, just off the top of his head, without even knowing the names of all the horses running? That's what I did in June 1970, when asked who would win the Belmont Stakes. Later, he sent me this affidavit:

"On Friday, June 5, Dr. Tanous told me that High Echelon would win the Belmont Stakes horse race on June 6. He did, returning $11 for every $2 bet. Larry Lonstein, Portland, Maine."

My news isn't always good, of course. One time, while I was on Larry Glick's show on WBZ in Boston, a caller asked me if the Red Sox would win the pennant. At the time, I was told, they were far in front. "No," I said, "they're going to finish second."

"Do you know who you're talking to?" Larry Glick asked me.

"I haven't any idea—a caller."

"That's Buddy LaRue—he's a Red Sox coach."

"Well, I'm sorry," I said. "But I don't see the Red Sox winning this year."

LaRue laughed. That year, the Red Sox finished second.

On December 31, 1972, I was in Portland, appearing—by phone—on WEEI, on the "Sports Huddle," a syndicated radio program, with Eddie Andelman. I was answering the usual questions—who would win this, where would that team finish, how many games would this pitcher win, how many touchdowns would this runner score.

During a lull in the phone calls, Eddie said, "What predictions can you make concerning the sports world?" It was eight twenty-two in the evening.

"Eddie, it's strange," I said, "but on December 24, I made the prediction that a famous man in sports was going to die, someone very well known, someone still active, not retired."

Suddenly, it was happening and, in my mind's eye, I was there, and the plane was falling, dropping, crashing into the sea, everything was black.

"It's crazy, it's crazy," I said. "It's happening right now." I didn't say it, it was too unbelievable. Roberto Clemente was dying at that instant and I was living his death.

"Well," Eddie said, "thank you for your prediction, Dr. Tanous. I guess it wasn't a very happy one."

"I know. But I can't control what I see."

The next day, the story of Roberto Clemente's death began to unfold in the newspapers. I later found out his plane had crashed at exactly eight twenty-two—the precise moment I was experiencing the event in my own mind, psychically.

I now have a letter in my files from WEEI confirming that I "correctly predicted the tragic death of a sports personality" on New Year's Eve, 1972, at the moment "Roberto Clemente died in a plane crash while on a mercy mission."

Helping the Police,
Psychically

It was inevitable, I think, that my long record of accurate predictions concerning famous people and important events would come to the attention of the police, the FBI, and victims of crimes (or their relatives), all of whom desperately needed information apparently impossible to obtain by conventional means.

And so, I have often found myself called in to help in criminal cases, to provide what information I could about how a crime was committed, who was the perpetrator, where the body (the money, the jewels, the car, or whatever) might be found.

To date, I've worked on about fifty criminal cases and I've been able to provide useful information in about forty of them. Unfortunately, some of my best work has been done in cases I cannot discuss, since they are not officially closed or otherwise resolved. I remember all too well what happened in the Debbie Horn kidnap case I worked on in 1969 while at St. Anselm's. My information was published in the newspapers prematurely and the kidnapers were frightened into killing the girl. So I intend to limit myself here to those cases that have come to a conclusion.

One of the first of these involved a stolen car. Let me quote from the victim's affidavit:

"On October 7, 1968, I had the unfortunate experience of having my car stolen. I asked Dr. Tanous if he could help me locate it. Without ever having seen my car, Dr. Tanous described it in detail, including its color, red. He told me that my car would be found—not that week, but soon after. Police would locate it, he said, on or near a tree-studded road. It would be stripped a bit, but mostly undamaged.

"Dr. Tanous then described two of the thieves. He said three people had been involved in the theft, but that he was unable to describe the third. My car had been stolen on a Monday. It was recovered little more than a week later, near Salem, Massachusetts, next to Route 93, a road studded with large, beautiful trees. The car was damaged precisely as Dr. Tanous had predicted.

"Later, the police arrested three men in connection with the theft. Two of them exactly matched Dr. Tanous' description! R.J., Manchester, New Hampshire."

Not all of my police cases have turned out so well. One time, the police asked me to help locate a two-year-old boy who had disappeared in Alfred, Maine. His mother swore she hadn't taken her eyes off him for more than five minutes.

I said the boy was kidnaped and he could be found in a "triangle within a triangle." This turned out to be a description of a certain nearby area, so named because of the road pattern. "Triangle within a triangle" was the place's nickname—though I'd never heard it.

The police made a careful, thorough search of the area, but the child was not found. I was asked to provide more information, but nothing of value came to me. Why I could locate a missing car, or even a dog, but not a child, I don't know. It doesn't make any sense to me, but that's the way it was.

I am convinced that some children who disappear and are never found have not been kidnaped by criminals—or even human beings. They've been taken, I believe, by residents of another planet. I know this sounds preposterous on first hearing, but I have several reasons for thinking it is so. First, many children disappear practically under the noses of their mothers, when they've been left unattended for only a few moments. Second, some disappearances have taken place in locations where no kidnaper could have known a child was there—in grassy, isolated back yards, for example. Third, others have occurred where a stranger on foot or in a car would have been spotted instantly by the child's parents.

The fourth reason is the most persuasive of all, I think. There are several documented cases on record of missing children who have returned to their homes (or been found at distant locations) years after they disappeared—with no memories whatever of what happened to them while they were gone. How could an ordinary kidnaping account for this?

Another time, I was contacted by a member of the Wolfeboro, New Hampshire, police department. They'd raided a noisy party of teen-agers near a lake and three boys had run off to avoid being caught. They'd used a boat, gone out on the lake, and vanished. Some said the boys had simply run off. Others thought they were dead.

I had the definite psychic impression that the boys had drowned. I told this to the police, who began dragging the lake. Several months later, one of the boys' bodies was found. To this date, the other two have not turned up, but it is probable that they drowned, along with their companion.

It wasn't exactly a police case, but on another occasion, I was able to sense when an apparent disappearance had nothing sinister or fatal about it. On April 14, 1972, I was on a flight from Boston to Syracuse, sitting next to a man named Patrick Olski, of Liverpool, New York. We were discussing ESP in general when he asked me about a trapper who was lost in the swamp near Syracuse. At the time, the police were searching the river for his body. "I'd appreciate it if you could give me some information about his fate," Mr. Olski said. "My daughter is a friend of his daughter and I know the girl is pretty broken up about her father."

"Well," I said, "I can tell you that the man hasn't drowned. He is alive and well—but he's left the area."

Later, Olski sent me an article from the May 2 Syracuse paper. It read:

"Albert Pope, the Liverpool man believed drowned in the swamp on April 10 when his truck and muskrat trapping gear were found alongside a nearby road, has called his wife and told her he was in Iowa, doing landscape work. State police, the sheriff's Navigation Patrol, and several volunteer firemen and scuba divers searched the Peter Scott Swamp and the Oneida River for several days after he was missing. They found his boat and a hip boot in the swamp."

Still another lucky guess on my part? Possibly, it can be explained that way. But can a lifetime of such "guesses" be dismissed as nothing more than luck? I feel there was no luck involved at all. In my psychic mind's eye, I saw Albert Pope alive and well. It was no hunch—I *knew*. I know how strange this sounds, but it is so.

In 1972, I did something even stranger. When I was called in on a murder case, I not only located the victim's body, but I was also able to draw an accurate sketch of the man later convicted of the crime—though I'd never seen him or a picture of him.

An article in the March 4, 1973, *National Enquirer* described the whole story and I quote from it here:

> The incredible performance of psychic Alex Tanous has convinced Chief Herman Boudreau of the Freeport (Maine) Police Department of the value of ESP in solving crimes.
>
> "Nothing today is impossible—nothing!" exclaimed Chief Boudreau, in crediting Tanous with helping detectives solve the puzzling and hideous slaying of an eight-year-old Freeport boy.
>
> "This was the first time I had used Tanous in a case," Boudreau told the *Enquirer*. "But I have always felt there must be something to ESP.
>
> "I thought: A lot of big-town police experts listen to psychics, so why shouldn't the police chief in a little town do the same? I'd go to any lengths to solve a case. I'd listen to anybody if it would help. And Tanous did help us—tremendously. I would definitely use him again."
>
> Tanous . . . was brought into the murder case at the request of the parents and relatives of the missing boy, John A. Nason, who disappeared from his home last June 13 and was later found suffocated.
>
> "I wanted Tanous in on the case, too," Chief Boudreau noted. "I wanted to see if his 'thoughts' backed up what our investigation was showing."
>
> As it turned out, his thoughts not only backed up police suspicions, but led officers to the missing boy's body, the chief said.
>
> "We were concentrating on four key suspects at the time, though we didn't tell Tanous," Boudreau explained. "I took him through the apartment house where the boy lived, and

then drove him around the district. I did this several times, but whenever we left the apartment house, Tanous would say 'No, no,' and continue pointing back to the boy's home. So I took him back for another look.

"He just stood there and said that the boy was dead, that the body was in the apartment house—he couldn't tell exactly where, though—and that the body was wrapped in something and under something. Amazing—for that's exactly what we found later."

The next day, Tanous went to see Boudreau in the Chief's office. "He handed me a sketch that he said he had drawn in the car coming over," the Chief related. "When I saw it, I immediately pulled out a photograph of Milton I. Wallace, one of our suspects in the case. And you couldn't tell the difference. To someone knowing Wallace and seeing the sketch . . . well, they would have known they were one and the same person straight off," Boudreau said.

"What was really astounding," he added, was that "there was no way Tanous could have known about Wallace." Wallace, thirty-three, a Freeport shoe factory worker, lived just down the hall from the missing Nason boy.

"Of course," the Chief went on, "we had already talked to Wallace. He had a record—having served time for a sex assault on a seven-year-old boy—and we didn't like his story. But Tanous' sketch was one of the things that made me decide, on the ninth day of the investigation, to take a chance, and accuse Wallace of the crime. We went to Wallace's apartment and found the boy's decomposed body under a bed, wrapped in a blanket—just like Tanous had suggested. What he had told us had put us on the right track."

Wallace was convicted of the crime and sentenced to life imprisonment on December 15, 1972.

The impulse to draw a sketch of the murderer had happened to me as I was driving along the road. Something told me to pull over and start drawing and I did. I knew my psychic self was aiding me, guiding my hand.

When I finished the sketch, I drove to the police department.

Chief Boudreau was there, conferring with an FBI agent about the case.

"I know this sounds crazy," I said, "but I just drew a sketch of the murderer."

The FBI agent looked at Chief Boudreau and they both shrugged. Then I handed the sketch to the chief and his eyes opened wide. He opened the top drawer of his desk and pulled out a photograph and laid it beside my sketch. The resemblance was uncanny. Both Boudreau and the FBI agent were astonished.

I did something similar on January 1, 1973. A Canadian man was found unconscious on the floor of his building, outside his office. He was lying in a pool of blood, slashed across the forehead. Later, he died.

In his office was a newspaper whose front page featured my picture and my New Year's predictions. Evidently, he'd been reading the paper before he was attacked. Canadian authorities contacted me for help, through a newspaper reporter.

From my home in Maine, I relived the crime, sending myself to the scene and watching the whole thing. It's strange, I know, but I was able to see the face of the murderer. I made a sketch of it and took it to the Canadian authorities. It exactly matched a composite picture they'd drawn.

Sometimes, my visions come too late to be of any help. Several years ago, while I was a guest on "Meet the Press" at WGAN, in Presque Isle, Maine, I was being interviewed on the TV show when word came into the newsroom that an auto accident had occurred.

On hearing the news, one of the newsmen turned to me and asked, "Tell us, Dr. Tanous, what happened in this accident?"

"I don't know all the details," I said, "but I know it was a fatal accident."

After the program was over, the state police called into the station and wanted to know where they had gotten their information about the accident since none had been released. The state police were told it was a prediction I had made.

Later that evening, at the home of the station manager, I elaborated. I said, "Three people were killed in an accident. They were driving in their car when they hit a truck, which turned over and crushed them."

The information came to me psychically; it came as these things always do—as a thought that would come into anyone else's mind. Other people argue with themselves in their minds, or simply talk to themselves silently. I listen for thoughts that come to me and tell me things I couldn't know otherwise.

The next morning, the newspaper carried the full story. Three women had been killed, it said, when their car smashed into a potato truck, which turned over and crushed the car in which the women were driving.

In police cases, as with everything else I've done, I've had my share of partial successes—and total failures. The failures aren't very interesting. I was simply wrong. This does happen—not often, fortunately. But the partial successes show something is getting through.

Take the case of the late House Democratic Leader, Representative Hale Boggs of Louisiana. On October 16, 1972, Boggs and Nick Begich, Alaska's Representative-at-Large, disappeared on a flight from Anchorage to Juneau. Nearly seventy aircraft conducted an intense search over a fifty-six-thousand-square-mile area nearby for more than five weeks, but in vain.

I had publicly predicted that a congressional representative would be in a plane crash in Alaska, so I wasn't surprised when a man named Peter Dana, acting in an official capacity, called on me to help find Boggs.

I told him several things. First, I said the plane could be found fifty to seventy-five miles from Anchorage. I described the route it had taken and the general appearance of the area in which it could be found.

Second, the reason the plane went down was an unexpected snowstorm.

Third, there'd been no radio message from the plane after it got into trouble because the pilot had forgotten to change radio frequencies when he changed routes.

Fourth, the plane might have survived the snowstorm, except that it was overloaded.

I also asked Mr. Dana if something was wrong with the plane. I felt it had been defective in some way, even before the flight.

Mr. Dana didn't answer that question, but he had comments on all my other points. First, he said, what I had described was not the scheduled route of the plane, but a bad weather alternate.

Second, a snowstorm had hit the area, covering not only the original route, but also the alternate.

Third, the last radio message received from the plane was five minutes after it took off. Aviation officials had hypothesized they'd heard nothing further from the plane because the pilot had forgotten to change radio frequencies as he continued toward Juneau.

Fourth, as for the overloading, Mr. Dana couldn't say one way or the other.

Some months later, I happened to talk with an aviation expert who knew the pilot of Boggs's plane very well. He said that the pilot had been one of the best, able to handle even a violent snowstorm. Only engine failure or an overloaded plane could have caused the crash, I was told.

Since I was unable to locate Boggs's plane, I consider this only a partial success. Perhaps the plane was where I saw it was, but had long ago been swallowed up by the Alaskan wilderness.

Another "partial" took place in Cleveland, Ohio, in early 1973. I was doing "The Morning Exchange," a TV show at a local station, when I was asked to help find two young boys—one was six, the other seven—who had disappeared a month earlier.

I said that the boys were dead and that when they were found, their deaths would look accidental. But there'd been no accident. They'd been kidnaped—and later murdered—by two men. I said they'd be found not in the main part of the city, but in the outskirts.

At almost the same moment I was giving my report to the police, the boys were found dead near the city's outskirts, in a creek that had been searched earlier without result.

Police Lieutenant Jack Delaney theorized the boys had fallen into the creek upstream and drowned, but I am still convinced foul play was involved. How else can it be explained that the creek had been searched earlier and the children hadn't been found?

The above is just a sampling of the work I've done on police cases, and a very incomplete sampling at that, because of the need for silence in so many instances. I have many similar cases on file, some of them involving headline events, but I am duty-bound not to discuss my findings. Perhaps in another book, someday. . . .

Private Predictions

As a psychic, I've been privy to the most private thoughts of all kinds of people. They've brought me their worries, their fears, their hopes and their dreams. They've written, called, phoned in during radio programs, visited me at my home, and sent for me to visit theirs.

To meet their requests for information, I give several types of readings. In one, I answer a series of pinpointed questions, such as, "I am going on a trip. Will I have any accidents?" Once I was asked just this question by a man taking a trip West by car.

"Be wary of a tornado and of a big truck that has crossed the median strip," I told the man. "Be careful, keep your seat belt fastened." He encountered both of these hazards during the trip and credits my words of warning with saving his life.

In another type of reading, the subject asks no questions at all, but just sits with me. As I touch his or her hand, the information comes to me. In a third type, the subject need not be present. I don't even have to touch his or her letter. In this kind of reading, I astral-project, I leave my body, go into the future and see the fate of the individual in question.

Depending on my subject's needs, I concentrate on specific areas or I do life readings, in which I explore many different areas of a person's life, including job, family, friends, children, health, etc.

In addition to readings, I make predictions for people under very informal circumstances, sometimes quite casually. I always try to answer whatever questions are asked of me to the best of my ability.

People ask me about everything from the trivial to the profoundly important. Most often, though, they ask about members of their family—even before they ask about themselves. This was especially true when there were American troops in Vietnam. Many a mother or father asked about a son there.

For example, I was once asked to locate a young man who was in Vietnam. Mrs. Z.N., for whom I made the prediction, later recounted the incident in an affidavit:

"I told Dr. Tanous of a friend of mine whose daughter had a husband in Vietnam. It seemed this young wife had written her husband for three weeks and all of her letters were returned to her. In the meantime, she read in the newspaper where (his) outfit had had a severe accident—an explosion had occurred. As you can well imagine, she became very upset.

"I asked Dr. Tanous about this event and he said he could not see any danger or death concerning her husband, but he did say that the husband was well and had been transferred. This question was asked by phone, during an appearance by Dr. Tanous on a local radio program at about 9:20 P.M.

"Shortly after midnight of the same night, my friend called me and told me her daughter had a call from her husband. He said he was well and unharmed—and he had been transferred!"

The following is taken from a letter from Mrs. Joan Knowles, written on July 6, 1970:

"I am delighted to be able to write this letter telling you that your prediction to me has come true. On May 9, 1970, I asked you if my son who was in Japan would be all right. You answered that he would be and that you saw him coming home within sixty days. Exactly fifty-five days later, we picked him up at Westover Air Force Base in Springfield, Massachusetts. When you made the prediction, the possibility of his coming home was so remote I dared not even think of it."

And this comes from a letter from Mrs. Amy Crone, written on September 19, 1970:

"Last March at the Catholic Church in Yarmouth, where you gave a lecture, you told me that my son would be home in August. I am writing to let you know that you were absolutely correct. He came home August 18. There was no way for you to have possibly known except through your ESP."

One day, a woman and her sister came to my room after a lecture for a reading. They were worried about their brother. I'll quote from their letter, omitting the name at their request:

"My sister and I came into your room crying. My brother had killed his wife—or so it was said—and he'd been arrested in Europe (where they lived). I had to go there right away. You said, 'Your brother is not guilty. They want to do what they call a pre-trial in the service. They'll find him not guilty and he will come back home.' Later, I found out that you were exactly right. He was being examined in Germany at the very time you were talking to us."

Another time, a woman introduced me to her son after a lecture. "This is Allen," she said, "and he's going to Vietnam tomorrow— for the third time."

"No," I said. "He is not going to Vietnam."

"What?" she said, excited. "Really? I don't believe it!"

"You'll find it's the truth," I said. "He's going to leave the Army."

"Mom, here are my orders to go," said the boy. "There's just no way I'm not going. All of this predicting is foolishness."

The next morning, as he was packing to leave, Allen's father had a heart attack and was rushed to the hospital. The Red Cross contacted the Army, which gave him a leave to stay with his family. Shortly after, he was discharged from the Army.

At the time I made the prediction, I did not know his father was going to have a heart attack. But I was sure he wasn't going to Vietnam. How did I know this? I don't really know.

A couple of years ago, while I was appearing on a radio program, a Mrs. Masters called me. "Dr. Tanous," she said, "my son left this house fifteen years ago. He left his wife and his children and we haven't heard from him since. In fact, his wife has since gotten a divorce and remarried. I don't know whether he is dead or alive. Can you tell me anything about him?"

I could tell her nothing on the air, but I later came to her house for a personal reading. Within five minutes, I'd told her that he was alive and in what city he could be found. She found out his address through telephone information, wrote him and was able to re-establish contact.

In recent years, many pregnant women have come to me and asked me to tell them the sex of their expected child. Since the odds that I could simply guess correctly were fifty-fifty and not enough of a challenge, I often went further, predicting birth dates, birth weights, etc., in addition to sex.

To date, I'd guess that I have predicted an expected child's sex about six hundred times. About 5 per cent of the time, I've been wrong. I've also had excellent success with birth dates and weights.

On one occasion, I told a pregnant woman that her baby would be born with red hair—though both parents were brown-haired. I was correct.

Another time, I was asked about a baby on the way and I saw there was something wrong—that they'd have to be extremely careful in the delivery. The mother told the doctor, but he pooh-poohed the idea.

When the time came to give birth, the doctor discovered the baby's umbilical cord had been wrapped around his neck. A Caesarian was needed to save the child's life.

Here are some more examples of correct predictions about babies, quoted from letters sent to me:

"Just thought you would like to know that your prediction on the sex and date of our baby came true. Must admit we were surprised, and so were a lot of other people. Thank you for your prediction. Bob and Claudette Perrigo."

"In the spring of 1970, you told me that I would have a healthy male child on December 18, 1970. I delivered a perfect boy at 3:07 on December 18. Thank you. Mrs. T.M."

"I wrote you when I was pregnant and you said it was to be a boy born in late April or early May (I was due in late March). My *son* was born *April 25*, 1970. Thank you. C.A."

I have many more of these letters, but there's no need to be repetitive.

One day, one of the secretaries at St. Anselm's came up to me and said, "I heard that you can predict about birth. I'm due in about a month. Can you tell me what kind of child I'll have?"

"No, Pat," I said. "You'll give birth in ten days. It will be a boy, weighing seven pounds, two ounces."

Nine days later, she called in and asked to speak to me. "You know," she said, "I have all my bags packed for tomorrow. I believe in you."

"Pat, I haven't changed my mind," I said. "It's tomorrow."

The next morning, I woke up at 5:00 A.M. with a terrible stomach ache. I felt like I was in labor. But I went to school anyway. At a quarter to twelve, my stomach pains suddenly ended. At that moment, I later found out, Pat gave birth to a boy weighing exactly seven pounds, two ounces.

How did I know, with such precision, exactly what was going to happen? I wish I could say.

Many of my readings have involved matters far less important than life or death. In fact, some of the questions asked of me have been really trivial. But I've always tried to answer. This is especially true during my lectures, when members of the audience have asked me to demonstrate my abilities.

Once, in Manchester, New Hampshire, a young man challenged me. He later wrote me a description of the incident, which I quote here:

"I said to Dr. Tanous, 'On my intramural shirt (at home), I have a number. What is it?'

"You answered, 'I see a three as the first number. Now, I can't see the second number. Wait—it's a zero. The number is thirty.' That was absolutely correct. R.J., Manchester, New Hampshire, November 1968."

The next year, Bob Ridge, of Portland, Maine, asked me about his upcoming insurance exam. I'll let him describe what I said:

"I asked Dr. Tanous: when I take my insurance exam, will it be in Portland or Augusta, how many questions will it have, will it be subjective or multiple choice, and what will my mark be?

"His reply: You'll take the exam in Augusta, there will be 100 questions and it will be multiple choice and you'll get an 87.

"Sure enough, it was in Augusta, 100 questions, multiple choice, and I got an 88."

Mr. Ridge goes on to tell of another prediction I made for him:

"I never had a car in my life. My wife and I thought often of it, but never could manage it. One day, while Dr. Tanous was talking to my wife on the phone, he said, 'You'll have a car in your driveway by Sunday.' This was Wednesday night. I laughed at my wife when she told me. I'll be darned—in about half an hour, my oldest daughter came in and told me the man across the street was selling his car and said, 'Why don't you get your father to buy it?' On Saturday night, the car was sitting in my driveway."

Most people, if they had made such a prediction, and it had come true, would have considered it coincidence. I would be willing to consider my own prediction a coincidence—if it weren't for the fact that I've made hundreds of similar predictions and had them come true. In my opinion, those who are quick to call an unusual occurrence—their own personal experience—a coincidence may be dismissing what is actually a psychic event.

People have often asked me why I don't spend a lot of time at the race track, the gambling tables, or with my stock broker, piling up a fortune. There are two reasons. First, money isn't really that important to me. My needs are modest and I've always managed well enough. Second, I've always had the conviction that my gift was given to me for the benefit of others, for those who really need help.

Sometimes, the aid I give is small, important only for the moment. For example, on one occasion at Thornton, one of the secretaries in the office had lost the only key to a room. "Can you tell me where it is?" she asked.

"I see a bunch of envelopes," I said. "I see a newspaper—not here, at your house."

"Of course!" she said, startled. She jumped into her car, went home, looked among a bunch of envelopes under a newspaper, and returned with the key.

"That was weird," she said, "really weird."

Another time, a woman called me and told me she'd lost a large sum of money. "I'm afraid I threw it out," she said.

"No," I replied. "You've put it among some papers in a small black container. It's lying in a drawer."

She searched her drawers and couldn't find it.

"It's there," I insisted. "I can see it."

A few months passed by and the woman called me again. She was sure the money was gone forever. Then, one day, she was cleaning out the drawers in her desk. She dumped one of them out and there, amid a pile of papers, was a small black billfold. And in the billfold was the money.

How do I know such things? How do I see them? I have no precise explanation, though I do have a general idea. But more about that later.

In another case, a woman wrote and told me she'd just lost her fine china. "It's in some boxes," I told her. "Look under some newspapers."

"I've already looked everywhere," she said. But she looked again, this time among some boxes, under a newspaper. There was the china.

A similar thing happened to me in the offices of the American Society for Psychical Research, in New York City. Fannie Knipe, executive secretary for the society, was looking for a two-page invoice which was always sent in triplicate. It couldn't be found anywhere.

"Give it a try, Alex," she asked. "If anyone can find it, you can."

"It's in there," I stated, pointing to a two-drawer filing cabinet near her desk. "The top drawer." Fannie opened the drawer that must have contained thousands of pieces of paper. I ran my fingers over the edges of the papers—just as I had run my fingers over the edges of some phonograph records as an eighteen-month-old child. Then I stopped.

"It's right here, Fannie," I said.

She pulled out the folder and inside was the lost invoice. All invoices were kept in her desk file drawer, not in the filing cabinet, which was used to file correspondence and important documents.

One day, while at my home, answering letters, I received a call from a woman who had lost her dog and was very upset about it. I told her what I could and, as a result, the dog was found. Later, she wrote me about the incident:

Dear Dr. Tanous. On November 23, 1970, our boxer dog disappeared without a trace. This was extremely unusual, in as much as she would not leave our yard and was very shy around other people.

We spent the next four days constantly looking for her, day and night. Through a mutual friend, I was able to contact you and ask your help in finding our dog. At that time, you made the following statements:

1. Our dog was alive and we would get her back.
2. We lived on a north-south road.
3. Our dog was picked up by three young male people.
4. She would be found in a northerly direction from our home, ten or less miles away.
5. After naming five towns to the north, you suggested we concentrate on the Bowdoin, Maine, area.
6. You described a house that you associated with our dog.

My husband and I now make the following statements with the greatest of pleasure:

1. We found the dog alive and well on December 7, 1970.
2. The street we live on *does* run north and south.
3. Someone had to have taken our dog to another area as she would not wander away under any conditions.
4. We found her about seven miles away in a northeasterly direction.
5. She was located—dead center—in the town of Bowdoin, Maine.
6. Our home fits the description of the house that you kept associating with our dog.

Words cannot describe how thankful we are to you. . . . Gratefully yours, Agnes and Bill McGoey, Lisbon Falls, Maine, December 10, 1970.

As I've said, one of these predictions might be considered a coincidence. Even two might be called nothing more than lucky guesses. But hundreds? Each of the cases I've described here and elsewhere in the book can be documented either through affidavits written by those involved or by witnesses, or by tapes taken directly from radio or television broadcasts on which I appeared. The details of a number of these cases have been filed with the American Society for Psychical Research in New York and this information is available to qualified researchers in the field.

The same is true of my work in the health field, which I feel is even more remarkable, even more inexplicable in some cases than my private predictions.

Psychic Diagnosis
and Healing

All of my life, it seems, I've had an unusual sensitivity when it came to matters of health. I've described many occasions when I've known a person was going to die before he did.

As I became more and more involved in private readings, such things continued to happen.

When I was living in Manchester, New Hampshire, a young woman from Gray, Maine, wrote me about a man she was seeing. I had a sense that he would die, but I didn't have the heart to tell her so directly. Here's how she remembers it:

"You told me in reply to a question concerning the man I was keeping company with that you couldn't see any future with this man for me. He was found dead Sunday morning, beside his bed, of a heart attack. Sincerely, Florence Wilson."

One May I was reading "auras" for several people, in New York. When I came to one young man, a friend of mine, I saw the aura of death about him. I said nothing at the time. Later, when he pressed me, I told him what I had sensed.

"Be very careful," I said. "Otherwise, something bad might happen to you." In August, he was killed in a horrible automobile accident.

Afterward, I talked to the young man's parents and revealed the prediction I'd made. They were bitter about the whole thing. They felt that if I hadn't made the prediction, he wouldn't have died. But

I know I wasn't the cause of his death, only the bearer of bad tidings. I wished then, as I often had before, that there'd been no bad tidings to bear.

Another time, a woman wrote me to say that her husband wasn't feeling well. "What do you see ahead for him?" she asked. Once more, I saw death. And since the woman had asked the question so directly, I decided to answer directly. I told the woman what I saw, that her husband had brain cancer and would die of it. Let me quote from her letter:

"I am writing for your files in regard to a prediction you made about a malignancy in my husband which you said would end his life. Eight months after the prediction you made, my husband was dead of lung and brain cancer. Sincerely, Mrs. Eleanor D. Murray, South Portland, Maine."

When people ask questions about themselves, health is often the subject. It was through questions about health that I found I could diagnose disease.

In Manchester, New Hampshire, I met a woman who had a rash covering both hands and arms. Local doctors had tried everything without success. I told her that she needed tar soap treatments and that she should go to the Lahey Clinic in Boston, where I had gone for years. If she did, I said, she would be cured in short order. She went to the clinic, as I suggested, and I saw her about three weeks later. She was completely free of the rash.

Was this coincidence? Had I merely picked up a bit of medical knowledge and applied it at the right moment? Maybe so. But how then do you explain this diagnosis?

"Dr. Tanous told me that I had had a major abdominal operation within the past two years and he was right. I'd had a partial gastrectomy. Since then, I have had occasion to ask other questions of Dr. Tanous. He has been right in his predictions. During this time, I became ill—had abdominal pains—and had occasion to see at least four doctors. Dr. Tanous told me it was pre-menopausal symptoms and should be treated as such. The doctors did not seem to agree. I went through many miserable experiences until finally my husband, Bob, was told by Dr. Tanous to seek out another doctor and tell him of the conditions. This Bob did and finally a series of hormone injections began to make things shape up. If only I had followed his advice, I believe I could have avoided much misery. Yours truly, Mary Ridge, Portland, Maine."

Another time, a woman wrote me about her son. He had been diagnosed as retarded and doctors had recommended he be sent to a school for retarded children. She asked me if I could tell her anything about her child. "He has touched this letter," she said. Somehow, I can't explain it precisely, I received vibrations from the letter. I wrote her back, saying that the boy had been misdiagnosed. Several months later, she wrote again:

"Dear Dr. Tanous. This is really a thank you note for answering my letter. I wrote you regarding our son Peter who had been diagnosed as mentally retarded. In my letter, I asked you if he really was retarded. You replied he wasn't. Instead, you believed he was quite bright, but very immature and sensitive. You advised me to take Peter to Boston Children's Hospital for further testing. Well, in December, after waiting three months, Peter was tested at the hospital for three days. They confirmed what you had written to us! Sincerely, Mrs. L.V., Portland, Maine." (I have not used her name, at her request.)

This comes from another letter:

"The first experience I had with someone with ESP was ten months ago, April 30, 1970, when you spoke at the Beta Sigma Phi founders' day dinner at the Lafayette Hotel. You said, 'I can see you are going to have an operation,' after taking my hand. I thought you would like to know you were right. I had an operation on the first of August. J.A., South Portland, Maine."

On another occasion, I was speaking to a club in Manchester, New Hampshire. After my lecture, I shook hands with a man and told him, "Your heart is okay, there's nothing wrong with it." He looked at me bug-eyed. It seemed that he'd recently had a heart attack—which I couldn't have known. Later, I met the man at another club.

"You know, you're right. My heart is perfectly normal. I should have been satisfied with what you told me. But I consulted Dr. Paul Dudley White, who repeated what you had said, almost word for word."

In the summer of 1970, I attended a seminar on psychic phenomena in Memphis, Tennessee. There I met a lady named Burma

Waldrop. "I'm going to have an operation at Johns Hopkins," she told me, "but the doctors don't believe it will do anything more than relieve my pain. They don't think I'll ever be able to walk unassisted."

Looking out of the window, I said, "Burma, I see a lot of dark clouds for you. But the operation will be successful and you will walk again. I want you to look beyond those dark clouds and you'll see that the sun is shining. You will be well again." It happened as I had predicted. Many months later, I met her again and she was walking, without crutches, without a limp.

One day after a lecture in Manchester, New Hampshire, I shook hands with a lady and sensed immediately that something was wrong. Superficially, she seemed in the best of health. But somehow I knew that she had a cancerous cyst and that she required immediate medical attention. Reluctantly, I took her aside and told her what I sensed. I'm glad to say this story had a happy ending. Several months later, while I was sitting in a coffee shop in Manchester, eating breakfast, the same woman approached me.

"Do you remember me?" she asked.

"I do," I said. "How are you?"

"Thanks to you, I'm fine. When you shook hands with me, you told me that I was ill, that I had a cancerous cyst and that if I didn't go to see a doctor immediately, I would die. I didn't know whether to believe you, but I did go to see a doctor. The physical showed nothing. But X rays revealed a malignant tumor. They operated on me and removed it. I feel that you saved my life."

Perhaps the most remarkable diagnosis I've done was by phone, back in 1969. Fortunately, I have an affidavit from Mrs. Lenore Difiore, Akron, Ohio, which describes in detail what I said:

> To whom it may concern: This letter is in regards to a phone call I made to Dr. Alexander Tanous on October 31, 1969, a Friday, around 10:30 A.M. In this phone call, predictions were made by Dr. Tanous about my mother's forthcoming surgery that morning and these are the results of those predictions:
>
> The following questions were asked:
>
> 1. Q. Is it cancer?
>   A. No.

2. Q. What is it then?
    A. It's a type of fungus.
3. Q. Will she be all right?
    A. Yes, she will have much pain, but will be fine.
4. Q. How long will she be in the hospital?
    A. She will be in intensive care a few days but will spend only about ten days in the hospital, no longer than two weeks.
5. Q. Will they have to take out any of the lung?
    A. Yes, but only a small section of the upper right lobe.
6. Q. How long will she be in the operating room?
    A. Not long, less than two hours, one hour and forty-five minutes.
7. Q. What was the cause?
    A. Possibly from an old infection she was unaware of. There will be medication to follow.

The following is an account of the accuracy of Dr. Tanous' predictions:

1. The answer was completely correct. It wasn't cancer.
2. The answer was correct. It was a histoplasmosis granuloma, a type of tubercular fungus.
3. The answer was correct. She had much pain and is fine.
4. The answer was correct. She was in the intensive care unit three days and out of the hospital within ten days.
5. The answer was correct. They removed only a small section of the right lobe.
6. The answer was correct. The doctors were in surgery one hour and forty-five minutes.
7. The answer was correct. But it must stand as a possibility, for the doctor said the same thing but it was only his opinion, which could not be medically proved. And there was medication to follow for a one-year period.

The doctors were to do exploratory surgery on the right lung. Through X ray, they had found what they referred to as a coin lesion. The surgery was very successful. The doctor who performed it was Dr. Earl Shields. It took place at St. Thomas Hospital in Akron, Ohio. I state that the above is as true and accurate an account as I can correctly remember. Sincerely yours, Lenore Difiore, April 19, 1970.

Once, in an indirect way, I even diagnosed—or predicted—my own illness, one of the very few times in my life where my gift has helped me personally.

I'd just come back from Europe and was poring through many letters that had been held in my absence. Among them was a Blue Cross/Blue Shield application for major medical insurance.

For some reason, I picked the envelope out of the pile. "Sign it," my psychic self told me, "because you're going into the hospital."

"Which hospital?" I asked myself. "Maine Medical or Mercy?"

"Just sign the application. You're going into the hospital."

I fooled around with it for a while and finally decided I couldn't afford it. I tossed the application into the wastebasket and went to bed.

The next morning, I glanced at the wastebasket as I walked by and saw the application again. It practically talked to me. It said, "Pick me up and sign me and take me to the mailbox."

Well, how could I ignore my psychic voice? I did as I'd been told. About a month later, I collapsed with a 105-degree fever. I was taken to the hospital, where it was found I had a bacterial infection, which required an operation. (It was after this operation that I made the recovery-room prediction I wrote about earlier.)

Without the insurance, of course, the hospital and doctor bill would have been quite a burden. But my insurance covered most of the costs. I had my psychic self to thank.

It was a very short step from diagnosis to attempts at healing. I had already done this once, I believe, at Our Lady of Holy Cross Seminary, when I told a young man to throw away his crutches. Now, people were pressing me to try to heal them.

From the first, I adopted a policy to which I continue to hold: I believe in medicine. I believe that people who are sick should see doctors. I will not attempt to heal anyone unless they have first consulted a physician and undergone whatever treatment the doctor has recommended. I will treat people only when all else has failed.

The first time I consciously attempted a cure was in Portland, Maine, in 1969. Here's how the subject, C.C., remembers it:

"My foot got caught in a power mower in 1968. My veins and arteries were cut. My own physician sat there with tears in his eyes and told me that I would never walk again unaided. It got worse instead of better. After a while, it turned black. It looked like an amputation was going to be involved, eventually. When I was driven to your house, Dr. Tanous, I could barely make it up the stairs.

"Before I left, you shook my hand and you said, 'You will be all right, you will make it.' I felt a current from your voice, not necessarily the hand. It went right through, penetrated my head, went right down through my system. Within two or three days, there was a sudden movement in the foot and I was so excited I really was in ecstasy. Gradually, bit by bit, I got my full movement back. The coloring even came back. Before, it was like an absolute hard piece of wood, no movement whatsoever, no matter how much I had wanted it, and I did want to walk.

"I was disabled almost a year before I saw you. The healing was absolutely phenomenal. . . . Sincerely, C.C., Portland, Maine."

In Memphis, I tried again. A woman who had been blind for many years came to me. I passed my energy to her and she began to see light and shadow. A woman with arthritis, who had not moved her fingers without pain for years, was able to peel potatoes after I saw her and touched her.

Back in New England, I continued to attempt healings. After one lecture, a woman who had suffered from migraine headaches for twenty-five years came up to me. I touched her and passed my energy into her. Months later, we met again and she told me she hadn't had a headache since.

Another time, a man came to me who had suffered from a backache for years. I touched him, gave him energy, and he suddenly stood up straight. He said he was completely free of pain for the first time in his memory. A similar thing happened with a man who had stomach ulcers.

Once, a woman with a broken arm—it was in a cast—came up to me after I lectured at Waterville, Maine. I didn't say I was going to heal her. I just touched her. And suddenly, a sensation went right through her. You could see it on her face.

I thought nothing further about the incident until the president of a bank—a man who knew the woman—told me what had happened to her after I'd touched her.

Evidently, when she returned home after the lecture, she felt that her arm had healed and she ripped off her cast. The next day, according to the banker, she went to her doctor—who bawled her out for removing the cast, but found her arm totally healed.

After telling me this story, the bank president revealed the real reason for his visit to me. He had a stomach ulcer which had resisted medical treatment. I touched him, as I had touched the woman. His pain disappeared. Later, doctors were unable to find any trace of an ulcer.

A similar thing took place in Scarborough, Maine, in May 1973. There, I saw Mrs. Virginia Bowser. She had an ulcer for six years. Her question to me was, "Will I continue to have stomach trouble?"

I said, "I think I can help you." I took hold of her hands and said that I could feel the exact location of her pain. I sent my energy into her, with the hope it would help. Later, she wrote to me:

"I went home, time went by, I had absolutely no trouble. I take no medication now. I eat things I never believed I could eat. I feel wonderful. And I feel it is all due to you. As we held hands that night, I could feel a flow go right up through my arms into my body. I don't know how to explain it any other way. It was really like a miracle. Yours sincerely, Mrs. Virginia Bowser."

My files are filled with letters such as these. Here's a brief sampling:

"I am forever in your debt for curing me of my painful adhesions last March 1971. Less than one week after your healing, my adhesions were gone. Ada Helen Hayes, New Hampshire."

"I want to express my gratitude for the healing I received on February 16, 1971. My leg, previous to this healing, was a source of pain to me for six years. I was told by a physician that I had phlebitis. Within a week after the healing, the pain and hardening of my leg ceased. I have not been troubled by it since that time. Andrea L. DeMers, Massachusetts."

"I met you at the International Psychic Seminar held in Memphis in July. At that time, after four or five other psychics had laid hands on me—without result—you took both of my hands and immediately some magnetic force passed into my arthritic hands and almost immediately I could open and close my hands easily and without pain. This I had not done in years. T.J., Memphis, Tennessee."

An unusual example of my ability to heal took place in upstate New York. While I was there on a lecture trip, a woman called me and described a problem her daughter was having. For two and a half years, she'd been unable to work, or even leave her house. She felt safe only at home. She'd seen a psychiatrist, but he hadn't been able to help.

The girl's mother asked me if I could transmit some of my energy to her daughter by phone. I said I would do my best. Soon afterward, I heard from the mother again. Within a few days of our conversation, the girl was able to leave her house. About a week later, she applied for a job—and got it. Since then, she'd been working regularly and leading a normal life, apparently completely cured of her abnormal and paralyzing fears.

I had another quite similar case in Maine, involving a young woman named Jeannine Chaput. Much of what she has to say about our contact is worth quoting:

"The fact that I was sick is a sure thing—the fact that I am better is also a sure thing. There are few days that go by when someone doesn't tell me, 'My goodness, this is unbelievable, what you're doing.' I was afraid of glass, I was afraid of steel wool—the fears were there. I was afraid I was going to hurt somebody, I was afraid to be near people because I might bump them and cause them to have cancer. I was terrified of hospitals and giving birth to my children was a terrifying experience for me. This sounds silly, I know, but a lot of the things that I feared were silly things.

"Each time before I went out I had to take a bath, wash my hair, try to get out of the house without going near the hall closet, or the pill closet, be able to sweep into the car without touching anything on the ground. I saw a psychiatrist for two and a half years and, at one point near the end, he told me he couldn't do anything for me.

"After I had spent three weeks at home in bed, not daring to move, a friend called you. That Saturday night, you came and you said, we're going out in the car. Now that seems like an easy thing to do, but by golly, I could not for the life of me believe you were going to make me go out in that car. Well, I went. . . . We did, together, all those things I was afraid of. I was afraid of staples— you took a staple gun and shot them out the door. You made me go into the garage and go through the cans that were poisonous.

"Then, when you visited us, you said, 'You're going to make a big step.' I begged you to tell what it was and you said, 'You'll know.' Two weeks later, I was working. It was the best thing that could ever happen. Today, I work a forty-hour week. I do a lot of public relations work, am responsible for budgets, am a half-time substitute director of the office. I've even been to dances—you know I've always wanted to go to dances. I do all of these things only because you did it for me. . . ."

Was this psychic healing or psychological counseling? I think it was some of each. The important thing was the result. But I was recently associated with another case in which there could have been no psychological component. Again, I quote from a letter written to me:

"Four years ago this June, I discovered that I had a lump on my breast. I had a mastectomy and it was malignant and I had deep X-ray therapy. For three years, I thought everything was fine. Then I got pneumonia. I went in for X rays and they discovered I had bone cancer. I was beyond cobalt treatments, so they tried chemotherapy. My bones were deforming. I had lots of pain.

"Then I met Dr. Tanous and he shook hands with me and I felt the energy. He said my doctor would tell me that the cancer was gone. That was on a Saturday night. Thursday, I went to my cancer specialist and he did a blood test and said he was very happy with the result. There was no cancer in the blood. Now, people can't believe it when they see me walking and driving, without pain. P.C., Scarborough, Maine."

In all, I would say that have there been about one hundred instances in which my intervention has actually helped someone who was ill or injured. Of course, I have attempted to heal many hundreds of times. In some cases, I haven't been able to help, or my help has been only partial. The healing process is an interaction between myself and the subject, I believe. In some cases, I simply can't make contact. In others, the person is simply too sick for my energy to make the difference.

In my experience, however, it doesn't matter whether or not my subject is a believer or a skeptic, or whether or not he believes in God. He needn't share my belief. Whatever this energy is that cures and heals, it's universal. Exactly how it works, I do not know.

Psychic Photography
and Other Strange Happenings

Whenever I'm around cameras—TV cameras, movie cameras, still cameras—strange things happen. The cameras malfunction, the film goes bad, flashguns won't fire.

When the cameras do work, they frequently produce some strange results. Sometimes, I'm missing from pictures taken of me, though the background is present. Other times, odd things appear on pictures taken of me, objects that weren't in the room. On other occasions, I have taken pictures myself and had them developed only to find images that weren't visible to the naked eye—energy forces, ghostlike figures, and other weird images.

My photographic troubles began innocently, if strangely. When I visited Memphis, Tennessee, for that psychic seminar in 1970, a professional photographer attempted to take some pictures of me but his camera wouldn't co-operate. Both the shutter speed and the lens aperture settings changed, without human intervention—though neither setting worked automatically.

This is how photographer Elbert W. Creed remembers the incident:

"On two separate occasions, while photographing Dr. Tanous, the f-stop (of my camera) was found at $f11$. This was discussed after the first time with observers . . . who checked the f-stop at $f5.6$. Then, after taking the picture, the f-stop was found at $f11$, as checked by observers. . . .

"I am a commercial photographer and when on camera, it is not unusual for me to shoot over five hundred pictures a day, which means speeds and *f*-stops are checked frequently. Elbert W. Creed, Memphis, Tennessee."

Another witness recalls the speed changes:

"In observing the camera setting, at 1/250th of a second, after several direct pictures of Dr. Alex Tanous, the speed ring rotated to 1/60th of a second. M.S., Maine."

Why did this happen? I have no explanation for it. Nor can I explain why I break cameras.

On August 26, 1971, I broke the camera of T. J. Caramadre, a Utica newspaper reporter, who'd come to cover a lecture I was giving at Clinton, New York. I warned him it might happen, but he went ahead with his picture-taking.

"Dr. Tanous is a man of his word," Caramadre later wrote in the Utica newspaper. "The camera ceased to work. Whether the equipment was on the verge of a breakdown probably will never be known, however [it] would appear that delicate photographic equipment is not worth being risked against [his] psychic power."

The first time this happened, I admit, I thought nothing of it. Cameras do break from time to time. But it happened again and again, always when I was the subject. I finally had to ask myself why. My psychic nature was the only reasonable explanation.

At one of my lectures, I told a man he should be careful taking my picture, because I might inadvertently break his camera. He pointed the camera at me and pressed the button. Nothing happened. He tried again, with the same result. The camera was broken. A year or so later, the same thing happened at Bloomsburg State College in Pennsylvania.

Another time, I made a reporter-photographer's flashgun go off, even though he hadn't triggered it. He wrote up the incident in the Rumford Falls (Maine) *Times*, on March 30, 1972:

"Dr. Tanous informed Pat Milligan backstage that he would make this photographer's flash go off without the trigger being touched and so it did when the camera was being focused."

On another occasion, I was lecturing when a man in the audience rose to take my picture. I said, "You don't have to snap the shutter

—I'll do that, from here." And I did what I promised, to his amazement.

How did I do this? I don't know. I just had a feeling I could.

A number of times, cameras have apparently worked, but the pictures taken of me didn't turn out. In the summer of 1973, someone took an entire roll of pictures of me as I lectured at Mary Baldwin College in Staunton, Virginia. The film turned out blank.

A couple of years earlier, I did a TV show for Channel 5 in Bangor, Maine. When the tape was played back, the picture was practically obliterated by lines. I told the engineers it was my fault and I apologized. They scoffed—though they admitted such a thing had never happened before.

Only on the second try were we able to complete the taping without incident. Since then, I've done many shows on tape for this channel and something seems to happen almost every time.

And it doesn't only happen at Channel 5. Something similar happened when I taped another TV program, this one for Channel 67 on Long Island, New York. I told the producer, Bill Chu, he wouldn't be able to photograph me that day, because the camera wouldn't work. I just had a feeling something like that would happen. He laughed and went ahead with the program.

Immediately afterward, we checked the tape—at my suggestion. It was totally blank. Mr. Chu couldn't believe his eyes. The equipment had functioned perfectly just before I was interviewed. When the tape turned out blank, the equipment was tested again. It functioned perfectly.

Craig Worthing recalls a couple of similar instances:

"The first time Alex and I did a TV show—back on Channel 13, in Portland—we couldn't get one of the cameras to focus. And we had only two cameras.

"Now you may say, that happens all the time. Well, it doesn't happen all the time. Those cameras cost eighty-seven thousand dollars new. They're expensive, important equipment and the stations take very, very good care of them. It's very rare that something goes wrong with them.

"Yet it happened when I did a TV show with Alex on Channel 13. We did five shows on Channel 20 and it happened three times.

Sometimes, it has happened to more than one camera at the same time.

"I suppose you can call this coincidence. I won't argue that. But is it coincidence that it always happens when Alex is around?"

Something even more peculiar happened in spring 1974, when I was with freelance writer Joseph F. Goodavage, who was doing a story on me. Here's how he remembers it:

"On March 29, 1974, during an interview with Alex Tanous, I took a series of black and white Polaroid pictures of Dr. Tanous with flashcubes—eight in all. Of these, two clearly developed negatives (which were identical in quality to the negatives that produced clear pictures) yielded completely blank positives. In view of the fact that the timing, temperature, and general conditions were virtually identical in developing each picture, it struck me as something of a paradox. I can find nothing in the photographic literature to explain the failure of the emulsion."

A similar incident took place in the summer of 1973, at the American Society for Psychical Research. I was in a small room with two photographers, Leonard Barcus, an optical physicist who had done a great deal of work for NASA, and Ann Johnson, the ASPR's staff photographer.

Having heard of the odd things that happened to me while I was being photographed, Mr. Barcus and Miss Johnson were doing an experiment to see if unusual results could be produced with low-light photography.

As a result, the room was illuminated by a single candle. Mr. Barcus had loaded his camera with Polaroid film and installed his fastest lens, a custom-made model that opened up to f87. It was fully capable of taking pictures in a room lit by only one candle. Miss Johnson was using infrared in her camera.

I lay down on the couch near the candle and Mr. Barcus and Miss Johnson started snapping away. In most of the pictures, I am visible, faintly illuminated by the candle. But on one, I disappear—while the candle stays lit! And in another, the candle and I both vanish. This is true both of the series of photographs taken by Mr. Barcus and of those taken by Miss Johnson. Other witnesses in the room have testified the candle stayed lit throughout the picture-taking session and I never left the couch. They saw nothing unusual while the pictures were being taken. The inexplicable effects were visible only photographically.

On three separate occasions, I visited Leonard Barcus at his home, for picture-taking sessions. On two of these, I produced what Mr. Barcus said, without doubt, were paranormal pictures. I'll let him tell what happened.

"Al would take pictures using the wink light on the Polaroid, aiming it at his face or into his eyes. Then, we'd take a series of pictures. I was there at all times, within a couple of feet of him, watching exactly what he was doing.

"Suddenly, instead of a picture, we would get a completely black shot, a blackie, exactly what you would get if you hadn't exposed the film at all, but had developed it anyhow.

"Then, there was one picture which had a series of light streaks across it—just as you might get if you'd taken a picture of venetian blinds somewhat out of focus. The light streaks had a very definite pattern.

"But there are no venetian blinds or anything similar in the room. I can't conceive of anything optical that could have done it.

"There were no more pictures of light streaks that night, but there were several other blackies. Blackies could be caused by a shutter malfunction. If the shutter didn't trip and the film was pulled out of the camera, then examined after sixty seconds of development, a completely black picture would result.

"But in this case, there was no shutter malfunction. The shutter release tripped the flashbulb, as usual. Pictures taken before and after the blackies were normal. I've never had a blackie with the camera at any other time. So there's no doubt in my mind that these were paranormal pictures."

On another occasion, Vera Feldman, an ASPR researcher, contacted people who did a series of pictures of me in the dark to see if they could capture my spirit leaving my body. When developed, they "showed umbrella-like swirls" (of light) and "some reverse effects: black spots which extended over the picture frames." Said Miss Feldman, "I feel it's very exciting."

I find it exciting too, though I cannot explain why it happened or what it means.

The strangest pictures ever taken of me, I think, were part of a series of experiments conducted by three Boston doctors. In an effort to capture on film my solidifying of light, they took me into a completely empty black room and began snapping pictures with several Polaroid cameras.

Much more appeared on the pictures than any of us had expected. My face could be seen, barely visible. Also visible were a bed, what appeared to be a coffin, a ball of light hovering over my shoulder, and a white blotch shaped exactly like a hand. And remember, there was nothing in the room at the time except myself and the three doctors. Yet picture after picture showed objects invisible to the eye. Why? I have no idea. I find it mystifying, but profoundly exciting.

The doctors have requested anonymity, so I can't publish their affidavits. However, they did give me several of the many pictures they took. I sent three of these pictures to Dr. Jules Isenbud, an expert in psychic photography. He found them inexplicable, outside the normal workings of the photographic process, and thought that they looked possibly paranormal.

In addition to being the subject of some pretty strange pictures, I've taken some odd photographs myself. Two were taken on a trip to Europe. The more startling of these is of the inside of an elaborate Russian church. To the right, in front of a row of pews, is the ghostlike figure of a woman, cut in half. When I first saw this picture, I was convinced it was nothing more than a double exposure. Closer examination showed everything else to be clear and sharp, however, with no sign whatever of a double exposure—except the woman. The other odd picture I took in Europe was of the front entrance to Beethoven's home. It appears to be entirely normal—except for a large white ringlike image in the doorway. I have no way to be sure, but I feel this is Beethoven's spirit.

The third of my strange pictures was taken at Salem, Massachusetts, in a house associated with ghosts and witches. My picture shows the fireplace in the living room. And in the photograph, on the wall above the fireplace, are two clearly visible Indian faces, one male, one female. Neither is visible to the naked eye.

I am sure I have taken other paranormal photographs, but I've thrown them out, thinking they were nothing more than camera or darkroom malfunctions. Strange-looking but perfectly explainable photographs are commonplace. Everyone gets them from time to time. Most are nothing more than double exposures, film accidentally struck by sunlight, or darkroom errors. But I am convinced genuine psychic photographs are far more common than most people think. For that reason, I urge you to examine carefully any strange-looking pictures you get back from the photo processers and have an expert look at any that can't be easily explained.

In addition to the unusual experiences I've had with cameras and photographers, I've had some mightly odd run-ins with other equipment, including tape recorders, watches, microphones, electric lights—even airplanes.

For example, at the same Mary Baldwin lecture which produced a roll of blank pictures "of me," I began by warning the audience the microphone might also go dead. At that moment, it ceased to function.

A few months later, I went to Anna Maria College in Paxton, Massachusetts, to give another lecture. Several members of the audience had brought tape recorders and they attempted to tape my lecture, even though I warned that my personal gremlin might make trouble. Afterward, I asked the people to check their tape recorders. None of them had worked. We then checked them out—with voices other than mine—and they worked perfectly.

On another occasion, I was doing a video tape for WGAN, in Presque Isle, Maine. Before we began, the engineers made a point of hooking up the controls so the tape I was making wouldn't be ruined by the show the station was broadcasting at the moment. When we played the tape back, the sound track of the show then being broadcast was audible despite the precautions, blotting out my voice and that of the man interviewing me, ruining the tape. So we did a second take. The engineers were astonished, but I wasn't.

One time, I was lucky enough for my gremlin to make repairs—after he'd done his damage. It was after I'd made a documentary film for New York University.

Here's how J.K., of the NYU film department, described it to me:

"We taped you—it was a brand-new reel—and we took it out and put it on the machine and it worked fine. D. (a member of the film department) went away and he came back and all of a sudden, the whole reel was—all the way around—it was completely bent in all these weird shapes. And there's nothing we could have done to it. We brought it to the tape people and they said, 'We don't know how it happened. It's not heat, because it didn't melt, it was just bent all the way around.'

"No one could understand how it happened because it was on the machine and the machine is not hot. So we put it away in a box and figured, oh, we'll just have to redo the whole conversation again. So a couple of hours later, D. went to show it to someone and it was perfectly fine. It was all straight. We had the tape in our possession the whole time."

D. has similar memories:

"The tape bent. It was as if you had taken the side of the reel and pulled it outward, into almost a cone shape. And for that to have happened, the reel would have had to have been away from the tape recorder. It couldn't have been sitting where it was on the reel spindle, it would have to be, say, seven or eight inches away and pulled with a tremendous force, a force great enough—under normal circumstances—to break the tape. The tape actually wound outward, further out from the center of the reel. It was at the point Dr. Tanous' voice was on the tape. It couldn't have happened naturally. I have used that machine for a year and a half and I've never seen anything like it."

To me, it was not particularly odd that something had gone wrong with the tape machine—though having the reel bent was a new one to me. What was really unusual was that it repaired itself. A few hours after the incident, the reel showed not the slightest sign of ever being twisted or bent. All I could do was wonder at the whole thing. I'd never attempted to damage the tape reel, mentally, nor had I tried to fix it. But I knew something about me had been responsible for both.

I've experienced that sort of thing—something going out of whack, then righting itself—on at least one other occasion. It happened on a Delta flight originating in Bangor, Maine, going to La Guardia. I got aboard in Portland, Maine.

I was sitting next to William Dobrowolski, executive vice president of Hanover Square Realty Investors in New York, talking about psychic phenomena, as I often do.

"I'm glad you're on the plane with me," Mr. Dobrowolski joked, "because now I know nothing can go wrong with the flight." I hear that kind of comment frequently, because people believe I wouldn't go on a plane that was about to crash. I hope they're right. So far, my psychic sense has never warned me away from a flight.

Just after Mr. Dobrowolski made his remark, the cabin loud-speaker crackled on. The pilot announced something was wrong with the wing and we'd have to land in Boston.

"No," I said to Mr. Dobrowolski, "we're going directly to New York."

"What do you mean?"

"I'm going to fix things."

I turned toward the wing and concentrated for about ten minutes. Fortunately, my seat was right over the wing, so I could see what was the matter: one of the flaps wasn't moving properly. Suddenly, I could see it begin to move smoothly again. By this time, we were over Boston. Once more, we heard the cabin loudspeaker come on.

"Ladies and gentlemen, this is the pilot again. Our difficulty has corrected itself, so we won't have to land in Boston after all. Since things are back to normal, we'll head directly for New York. We should be on time at La Guardia."

It wouldn't have really mattered if we'd been a little late. I keep a rather loose schedule, since I can't wear a watch. Why can't I wear a watch? Because I've had trouble with every watch I've ever worn. They stop, they run backward, they jump ahead—they do everything but keep even reasonably good time. And I'm afraid I affect other people's watches too.

On December 5, 1973, when I was speaking at the University of Maine in Bangor, I shook hands with Curt Mitchell, a student, and his watch stopped. It was one of those battery-operated watches. The battery was new. I tried to restart it, but I could not. I told the story at the lecture the same night and three similar watches stopped in the audience. At another lecture at Husson College, also in Bangor, I was telling the story, and the regular wind-up watch of a college official, who was listening to me speak, stopped.

When I began working on this book, similar things began to happen to the watch belonging to my collaborator, writer Harvey Ardman. His watch, a Bulova Accutron, stopped, went backward, skipped forward a day (it's a calendar watch), jumped back an hour, then ran again, quite accurately. The factory service center checked it out thoroughly and said it was running perfectly; nothing had ever been wrong with it. When Harvey told them what had happened, they laughed.

In addition to my effect on machinery, I also seem to cause lights to go haywire. On literally dozens of occasions, the lights have dimmed or gone off when I walked into a room.

While I was in Europe a few years ago, I switched on the lights in my Copenhagen hotel room. And then something in my head clicked. I can't describe it any better than that. The lights went off, though I hadn't switched the lights back off. In fact, the whole floor had gone dark. I called the service desk and they sent up an electrician—who found nothing wrong. The bulbs, fuses, and wires seemed fine. While he was studying the situation with a flashlight, the lights went back on.

Something even stranger happened at the American Society for Psychical Research. I was closeted with several researchers when the lights began to dim, on and off. One of the witnesses described it this way:

"The first time I saw it, I thought it was just a very common thing that we see in our lights in New York—some momentary lowering of the power and the light goes down for a second.

"But a sort of pattern developed. Dr. Tanous . . . would say, 'Well, now we are going to see something, I'm going to get more power.' And it did seem to follow this way. Each time, the lights dimmed. . . ."

The same thing happened when I visited a "haunted house" in upstate New York with a film crew. Father Alphonsus Trabold accompanied me. "As you walked into the room," he later commented, "at least one or two lights flickered."

I was talking about this ability at a high school in Machias, Maine, while raising funds for an anti-drug program, when someone in the audience asked me if I could put out the lights then and there.

"I don't know," I said, "but I'll give it a try."

I gazed into the lights in the room, trying to draw their energy from them, and I said, "Lights, *out!*"

Suddenly, the room went black. And not only the room, the entire school. And not only the school, the entire town! The blackout lasted about a minute. Afterward, I was interviewed by the local radio station. I could not explain what happened. But I was sure I had caused it. This happened on April 28, 1970.

Then again, I suppose it could have been a coincidence, a simple power failure, accidentally taking place at exactly the same moment I said, "Lights, *out*." But I'd hate to have to figure the odds against something like that.

At other times, I have shown the ability to move objects without touching them. Perhaps this is what happens when I play havoc with cameras and other machines. At Cheverus High School, my students and I put the cap of a ball-point pen on a book and I attempted to move it. Suddenly—I can't explain it—energy came out of my eyes and the pen cap moved a short distance.

The students said, well, maybe that was our imagination. They hadn't marked the spot where they'd put the pen cap. But when we took the cap from the book, we saw the spot was scorched. Why had this happened? I can't say.

Shortly afterward, I visited an art gallery with my niece. As usual, I was talking about ESP with some friends, my eyes focused on a nearby picture. Suddenly, the picture began to swing back and forth, violently, though it hadn't been my intent to move it. It continued to sway until I took my gaze from it.

Another time, at the American Society for Psychical Research, I moved a very heavy drapery without touching it, with every window and door in the room closed. A witness describes it this way:

"I am sure [the drapes] moved. I was very close. I sat right near the fold and four or five times, I observed them move. I saw a fold in the curtain, the very edge part of it, next to the wall, open up—just open right up against the wall. I am sure that what I observed was not optical illusion. Mr. Apsey, 11/11/69."

Recently, I walked into the office of Lee Sherwood, formerly an executive with "Monitor," the national radio program, and now with WMAQ in Chicago, and a row of big books on a bookshelf fell down. Until that moment, the books hadn't even wiggled. I didn't mean to release my psychic energy this way, but it happened anyhow.

The next time I talked to Mr. Sherwood was by phone. As he hung up, the books fell again. He later told me that someone rushed into his office, on hearing the crash, saw the books, and asked—with a wry smile—if Alex Tanous had just been on the phone.

Coincidence? Possibly. But the books have never fallen before or since.

Even separately, all of these things are remarkable, I believe. Taken together, they're astonishing.

The Psychic Light in My Eyes

All my life long, I've had a strange relationship to light.

It began in my grade-school days, when I learned to draw psychic images from the flickering flames of oil or kerosene lamps, and when I found I could see visions in the rays of the sun.

I felt then that I had established some kind of symbiosis with light. That's why Father Laplante's remark about seeing the past in a distant lightwave meant so much to me.

Through the years, I've had many reminders of the surprising, apparently mutual, attachment between myself and light. My ability to see through that illusory Navy beacon-landing system for aircraft carriers (at Fordham) is one example. So is my ability to turn off room lights.

Recently, this relationship has gotten much stranger—and much stronger. At least three different kinds of things have happened to me, truly astounding things:

· Time and time again, people have told me that as I lectured, I was surrounded by a visible glow, an aura.

· Continuing my experiments with light, I found I could absorb it with my eyes, then release it for all to see (and photograph) in balls of "solidified light."

· Challenging myself further, I discovered I could project not only balls of light, but actual images, images which could be seen by everyone in the room.

I know how completely preposterous these statements must sound to anyone skeptical of paranormal occurrences. Even those who are comfortable with the concept of psychic phenomena may find them difficult to accept without further explanation and documentation. I'm sympathetic to such feelings. No one finds any of this more astonishing than I do.

The first person to see an aura around me was Mrs. Barbara Meier, of Manchester, New Hampshire. Here is her affidavit on the subject:

"I have never seen him [Dr. Tanous] but what there is a mist around his head. For the first few times, I tried to believe it was a factor of my own eyes, but after having been at many lectures and at my own home with him, I can verify myself on seeing this always. Usually, it is a colorless mist, but occasionally tinged with blue and red rays. It surrounds his head completely to his shoulders, sort of in back of him. This . . . is a wonderful thing to me, as I have never witnessed such a thing in anyone before. Barbara Meier, Manchester, New Hampshire."

Others have also seen this. Here are some of their reports:

"Dr. Tanous rose to present the chief speech of the evening. As he began to speak, I noted that an aura appeared about his entire body. It should be noted that the wall behind him was blue in color. The aura, however, was a definite light green, somewhat reminiscent of that found in certain neon lamps. The aura was not fixed. At times, it appeared to extend perhaps two inches from his body and varied constantly from that distance to six or eight inches, something like a cold, flickering flame.

"My first thought was that I was tired and my eyes were playing tricks on me. So I closed them for perhaps one minute, then looked again at Dr. Tanous. The aura was still there. At the conclusion of the meeting . . . two persons came to me individually and reported that they had also seen the aura. When Dr. Tanous concluded his remarks and resumed his seat, the aura disappeared. This is all I know of the matter. Norman E. Leighton, December 7, 1969."

"At your lecture in Brunswick, I noticed a yellowish white aura around your head. I didn't mention it to anyone. Last night at [another] lecture, I noticed the same color aura around you and at times your silhouette moved across the back wall. It was fascinating to see. The aura could be seen only when you were on stage. My husband said he saw a colored aura around your head and thought it was due to his glasses. Mrs. C.R., Maine, January 14, 1971."

Evidently, others have also seen that silhouette from time to time, though they've called it by other names. An example is noted in this brief statement from a Cleveland, Ohio, woman:

"During your lecture on November 14, 1973, at Lakeland Community College in Mentor, Ohio, I was aware while you were speaking that I was perceiving your etheric double, observable on the stage. R.L., Cleveland, Ohio."

It wasn't as though people were expecting to see an aura about me, adjusting their perceptions to meet their expectations. A Maine woman attests to this:

"My husband and I saw you last spring and think you are remarkable. He could see light rays radiate from you, starting chest high and sometimes going far above your head and out to each side. He didn't know that other people have seen these lights, so he was a little nervous until I told him what I'd read. Diane Littlefield, Hampden, Maine."

In addition to my aura and my etheric double—that ghostly silhouette—others have seen a strange, blue-robed lady kneeling behind me, praying. Barbara Meier (Mrs. Frank Meier) was the first to see the figure. She described it as "a beautiful woman dressed in blue, with a mantle over her head, kneeling, praying for you."

I was astonished when Mrs. Meier told me this. I didn't know what to make of it. Then, not long after, it happened again. This time, the observer was a young boy who was attending my lecture in Maine, with his mother.

He told his mother he'd seen a lady in blue kneeling, praying behind me. His mother was quite upset at me. She was sure I'd caused some sort of emotional disturbance in her child. Only after she talked with Henry Gosselin, editor of *Church World,* who's heard Mrs. Meier's account of the same phenomena, did she calm down.

The aura, the silhouette, the praying, blue-robed lady are all remarkable. Even more astonishing, I believe, is my ability to project images and my ability to "solidify" light.

The best way to describe what I mean by "projecting images" is to quote from the affidavits of people who've seen me do it:

"To whom it may concern: Tuesday night, May 6, 1969, was a date which my wife and I shall long remember, for it was then that Dr. Alexander Tanous projected an image on the wall of our living room, through use of his powers of concentration.

"My wife and I, with Dr. Tanous, had returned from dining out that evening and were conversing in the living room of our home. My wife had just gone to the kitchen to prepare some refreshments when Dr. Tanous suddenly exclaimed that he felt an urge to attempt the image-projection feat of which we had been speaking. He indicated that he would attempt to project on the wall behind me and as I turned in that direction, my wife entered the room and stood in the doorway directly across from me.

"As I glanced towards the wall, an image suddenly formed on its surface with a suprisingly remarkable resemblance to the head and shoulders outline of a man. Thinking at once I had caused myself to see this through the power of suggestion, I blinked my eyes, shook my head and looked again—but the image remained in position.

"Not yet accepting the sight before me, I was about to blink once more when the image faded, disappeared, and then, just as suddenly as before, reappeared. It was at this moment that Dr. Tanous spoke, exclaiming elatedly that he had done it and asked if we had seen it as well. My wife was the first to answer and described exactly what I, too, had seen; it was only then that I fully realized what had happened.

"What had appeared on the wall was not a shadow nor a figment of my imagination, but an actual projection. . . . In order to allay as much doubt as possible among those who will certainly hear of this occurrence and raise questions, I make these notes while the facts of the matter are still fresh in mind and have been neither diluted nor embellished with the passage of time.

"The room had been softly lit by the glow of a lamp located on a table in the corner adjacent to Dr. Tanous. I sat across from him at the other end of the room. The wall was to my back, separated from me by a stairwell to the front entrance, with a decorative railing by its side. Some light reflected in from the kitchen. When the image first appeared on the wall, it seemed to be a glow of light, rather than a darkening of shadow, not at all as you would imagine an object casting a shadow, but rather an absence of shadow similar to the effect created . . . by a flashlight beam.

"What struck me as particularly noteworthy was the total spontaneity of the action—no preparation or conditioning, simply a matter of impulse and accomplishment. I also realized that although Dr. Tanous had indicated he would attempt this projection, at no time prior to doing so did he make mention of what form the image would take. My wife and I had no trouble concurring in all aspects of its appearance, location, and duration . . . which, although fairly briefly, was sufficiently long to be duly noted and recognized. Frank Meier, Manchester, New Hampshire."

Less than two weeks later, I did it again, under totally different circumstance.

"White visiting Mrs. A. at Mercy Hospital in Portland, Maine, I enjoyed the visit of Dr. Alex Tanous, who had also come to visit," writes Mrs. F.G. "Dr. Tanous said he would cast a picture on the wall, and as I looked up, I saw a square just light up, just a plain sort of outline of a frame, and it seemed to be illuminated. I looked away for a moment and blinked my eyes and again glanced back at the wall and saw that part of the square had faded. It was truly amazing. Mrs. F.G., May 23, 1969."

A few months later, I managed the feat again, this time in front of seven witnesses. We were all at the home of Mr. and Mrs. Edward Pawlowski. One of the men said jokingly, "If you start moving objects or making lights appear, I'm going to walk out." Until that moment, no one had even mentioned the idea.

Suddenly, light flashed from my eyes to a picture on the wall, framing it. Mrs. Pawlowski saw it first. Her face dropped and her eyes bugged out. Someone said to her, "What's the matter, Mary?"

And she turned to me and asked, "Did you do that, Dr. Tanous?"

"What?"

"I saw light flash across that picture," she said.

All at once, I began to shoot light up and down and in streams, in every which way. At one point, I caused a picture of a ship to appear to be sailing over a wall. It was like a fireworks display. And I couldn't control what I was doing.

But let the witnesses describe it, in their own words:

"On Saturday night, October 25, 1969, shortly after midnight, while Dr. Alex Tanous and five other people and my husband were all talking in our living room, I turned my head to say something to Mrs. Sylvia Allen and her husband and Mrs. Mary MacKenzie, and my eyes went to the wall in the corner. I saw the outline of a ship in light, a reproduction of the picture. I quickly took my eyes off it, as I was very frightened by what I saw. My hands were shaking. I couldn't believe what I was seeing, but I looked again and it was still there. I wasn't going to say anything, but I just had to ask everyone if they'd seen it.

"Dr. Tanous then immediately asked me what I saw and I told him. He said, 'Yes, I just projected that picture onto the wall.'

"After that, starting across the top of another picture and going all around it was a wide band of light framing the picture. In the corner of the room, a wide band of light starting from the ceiling extended down to the floor, flashes of light making like frames were everywhere in the area. The left wall was quite dark and the opposite wall very light. This went on from after midnight until almost 2:00 A.M. The band of light in the corner would not go away.

"Dr. Tanous said, 'I cannot turn it off.' Until he got up from his chair, put his hands over his eyes, and turned away from it, the light remained. After that, my fear had left me and I was very amazed at all that had happened. Mrs. Mary L. Pawlowski, Portland, Maine."

Mrs. Pawlowski's husband wrote this description:

"I realized my wife was in a state of fear. She said, 'Oh my Lord, did you see that on the wall?' At first, I refused to believe what I saw. But this is what I saw in the next hours: 1) a light from the top of the ceiling down the corner of the room to the floor, 2) the picture came out of the frame slightly, moving to the left and thus causing an effect like a double exposure, 3) the left wall became darker than the right side, 4) a small ship near the corner (of a picture) moved away from the picture and started to sail backwards— and that's when I yelled out, 'Oh my God, the ship is going backwards!' Edward Pawlowski."

A guest at the Pawlowski home saw it this way:

"On the evening of October 25, 1969, I was invited to the home of Mr. and Mrs. Edward Pawlowski to attend a meeting with Dr. Tanous and four other guests. Between the hours of 12:15 A.M. and 12:30 A.M. [Oct. 26], I saw a stream of bright light extending from the top to the bottom in the exact corner of the wall in the room we were in. For the next two hours, Dr. Tanous projected a series of images on that wall.

"There were two pictures on the wall, one large one on the left and a smaller one on the right. I saw Dr. Tanous light up the whole frame around the large picture. I saw him project the smaller picture frame on the right-hand side. On this picture, he projected the frame right beside the picture on the wall. Thereafter, the image jumped around on the wall. What I have written is true to the best of my memory. Ronald P. Allen, Portland, Maine."

After this incident, I contacted Dr. Karlis Osis at the American Society for Psychical Research, with whom I had worked in the past, and described what had happened. He asked me to visit the ASPR labs in New York as soon as possible.

On November 16, 1969, I attempted to project images or light beams on the walls of the ASPR labs. One witness, a Mr. Apsey, offers the following report of what happened.

". . . As soon as the lights were put on, I began to look at the wall. And I saw what looked to me like bright patches, like patches of bright cloud. I also saw streaks of light, not wider than a quarter inch. Sometimes, there would be one or two, but other times, there would be whole systems of them—groups of maybe eight or ten. They were side by side, parallel. They kept going on and off. Sometimes they just flashed. . . .

"Dr. Tanous tried to throw the light on the curtain and then I did see what looked like a bar, a relatively wide stretch of light, go horizontally across the curtain, a band of light six to eight inches wide. And it was solid. It didn't look the same color as the light on the wall, it looked more yellowish. The light on the wall also varied when I saw it. At times, it had a purple tinge. These patches of light stayed several minutes, possibly five or more."

The preceding is a transcription from a tape I made of Mr. Apsey describing what took place, shortly after the actual event.

As time went on, I developed a new ability. I call it "solidifying" light. As in the old days, it began when I "charged my eyes" by gazing into the light. But it was not a simple glance this time, nor was the light source as dim as the kerosene or oil lamps of my past.

When I "solidified" light, I stared, sometimes for ten or fifteen minutes, into the brightest light I could find—usually a photographer's strobe. I took its full glare, my face no more than three inches from the bulb. And then, I focused my eyes, and balls of light—visible to anyone in the vicinity—leaped out of my eyes. It was amazing, to me as much as to anyone.

It first happened in Memphis, when Elbert Creed was taking pictures of me on July 26, 1970. I stared into his flashgun, then focused my eyes. "A dancing light was observed on Dr. Tanous' hand by myself and others present," Mr. Creed writes. "The lights were turned off and exposures made which show the 'dancing lights.' Also, Dr. Tanous was changing the shape of the light rings emitted from the flash unit. This is a true statement to the best of my knowledge. Elbert Creed, Memphis, Tennessee."

In November 1970, I did something still more surprising. After a fund-raising lecture at Brunswick, Maine, I absorbed the light from a photographer's flashgun, then shot it out of my eyes and let it fall on the head of a priest who happened to be there. Three to four hundred people witnessed the incident, including the Reverend Edward O'Leary (now Bishop of Maine).

The light hovered over the priest's head, like a cloud or a mist. And it changed color, appearing mainly blue at first, then slowly turning green, yellow, orange, red, purple, etc. After a few minutes, it dissolved and disappeared. Everyone was overwhelmed by what they'd seen, myself included.

The next year, while doing a radio show with Craig Worthing at Cheverus High School, I gazed into a photographer's flashgun while he flashed it repeatedly, while more than 150 people watched. Then I stared into my outstretched hands. A large ball of light gradually coalesced in my palms and hovered there for several minutes. A photographer took several pictures of the phenomenon, which clearly show the light ball. Here's his description of the event:

"On May 17, 1971, at Cheverus High School in Portland, Maine, during a lecture by Dr. Alex Tanous, I took pictures of him while he isolated light. I used a Polaroid Model 450 camera with type 107 black-and-white film. I used just one role of eight pictures and captured three pictures of the isolated light.

"I'm employed by Camera Enterprises of Norwood, Massachusetts, so I am quite familiar with this and many other cameras. Peter Larsen, Falmouth, Maine."

Craig Worthing remembers the incident this way:

"In the audience of 150 people or so, 60 saw the light balls. Dr. Tanous would say, 'Now I'm holding it here, and I'm folding it into a square'—he was playing with the thing, as though it were a toy. And people would say, 'Oh yeah, now it's over your head, now it's down by the floor,' and so on. Afterwards, all sorts of people came out of there with Polaroid pictures that show the ball of light."

Two months later, I duplicated this feat in Utica, New York. Some two thousand people who'd come to hear my lecture witnessed the whole thing. Among them was a reporter from the local newspaper. This is how he wrote up the story:

"In solidifying light, Dr. Tanous' eyes suffer a severe light torture. A 500-watt bulb is flashed on and off, eight or ten times, only inches away from his eyes. The room is in total darkness. He then stares intently into his outstretched arms and shapes the form of a ball of light with his hands. Within seconds, a blue, misty ball of light appears there. At least a dozen Polaroid pictures taken of Dr. Tanous in total darkness showed the round ball of light.

"Dr. Tanous, in taking full exposure of light, was able to solidify it into a small ball of light that was evident to this reporter. It is similar to a person squeezing his eyes shut very tightly and upon opening them, seeing dots of light. But in this case, though the dots belonged to Dr. Tanous, others could also see them. There was no apparent harm done to his eyes—though the flashgun broke." The reporter here was T. J. Caramadre.

Craig Worthing was also present this time. He remembers the events of that evening this way:

"This particular night, people kept saying, 'Well, I know why people see this light. When you're flashing this 500-watt bulb into his eyes, it's just like looking into a real bright bulb—when you turn the bulb off, you see spots all over the place.'

"So we covered Dr. Tanous' head with a coat. The only person who could see the light was Dr. Tanous. Well, the light appeared and hundreds of people took Polaroid pictures of it. My two sons saw it, so did my wife. For some reason, I didn't. Maybe I was looking too hard.

"Everybody described it as a glowing ball in Dr. Tanous' hands. He formed it into squares, moved it around. He did it for at least forty-five minutes that night. And people were saying, 'I see it, there it is, now it's a square, it's over his head, it's over that lady's head.' Pictures and pictures and pictures and pictures were taken of it. My own boy said, 'There it is, don't you see it?'

"I saw nothing. I saw a black room. But more than one thousand people had to see it that night, because everyone in the place was aghast over what they saw. We got all kinds of pictures and I can tell you, I saw the ball of light in the pictures, all right."

The next year, I did something similar in my class at Thornton Academy—though in a far different way. For some reason, the class thought I was angry.

"No," I said, "I'm not. When I get angry, you'll know it—you'll see light coming out of my eyes and it will hit you."

Later in that hour, I did get angry, really angry. And I walked to the window and looked directly into the sun. Then I returned to my chair and looked at a girl in the class.

Suddenly, something clicked inside me and a ball of light flashed from my eyes to the back of the classroom and bounced back. This happened twice. Several students were petrified, both by the light and by the look on my face. They said I looked like a two-hundred-year-old man. It was the talk of the school for days.

People have often asked me if I could explain my ability to project images or to solidify light. I admit I have no satisfactory explanation. All I can say for sure is that my eyes have an odd affinity for light. Other than the usual eye tests, my eyes have never been studied by any competent authority.

However, on one occasion, I did look through a series of light filters with some colleagues. These filters blocked out all but the tiniest segment of the electromagnetic spectrum. A number of them were keyed to infrared and ultraviolet light.

We all looked through the filters, one by one. To everyone's surprise, I could see through many that were opaque to everyone else. What does this mean? I don't know. But I believe it and my ability to project images and solidify light are somehow related.

I don't know how or why I am able to perform these extraordinary feats, or what they mean in the larger scheme of things. But I feel image projection and light solidification may be a key to the ultimate understanding of all psychic phenomena.

Separating I From Me
and Myself

Man has always dreamed of someday being able to transport himself instantly through time and space, using nothing more than mind power. Most people consider this a fantasy, just one more unfulfillable wish. I do not.

Along with a small group of scientists investigating the paranormal—and some other psychics—I am convinced people can travel long distances, that they can go forward or backward in time—or both, separately or together—by doing nothing more than exercising their will.

My reason for believing this is simple enough: I've done it myself, literally dozens of times. I've done it in front of witnesses. I've been seen at distant locales while it was verified that I was at home. I've been detected by laboratory instruments in one place while it was known by all involved that I was in another.

I'm by no means the only person to have had such experiences. Many others have reported similar happenings in personal accounts, in scientific journals, in literature ancient and modern. In fact, I believe many people—if not most—have done things like this, usually without being aware of it.

For example, who has not experienced *déjà vu*, the uncanny feeling you've been here before, or done this before, or seen that before —when you know you haven't? What better explanation of *déjà vu* can there be than it is simply the memory of a brief mental trip through time and space?

Many terms have been used to describe these trips: bilocation (being two places at once); astral projection (the casting out and later retrieval of one's "astral body," a kind of energy or spirit entity); and out-of-body experiences or OBE (in which some relatively intangible part of a person leaves his body and returns).

Generally, scientists and psychics use the terms "astral projection" and "out-of-body experiences" interchangeably. Both refer to a phenomenon in which the "traveler" can see what's happening at a place far from his body, but observers cannot see him there—unless they, too, are psychic. "Bilocation" refers to the reverse: observers can see the "traveler" whether or not they're psychic, but he cannot see them—or, at least, he cannot retain the memory of seeing them, once he has returned from his "trip."

Though I've had both kinds of experience, there's much about them I do not know. I don't know how, exactly, I do what I do. I don't know why I'm able to "travel" this way on some occasions but not on others. I don't know the reason I've been given this ability, if there is a reason.

But I do know that the implications of this phenomenon, so far as mankind is concerned, are enormous. If a living man is able to detach part of himself, send it elsewhere, then retrieve it, might not a dying man detach part of himself and not retrieve it, leaving that part to survive him after death? Does such a thing happen automatically at death? But now I'm getting ahead of myself.

My first out-of-body experience took place when I was still a small child. That's what happened, I believe, when I jumped down those stairs, looked back up toward the top and saw my "other self," my "astral body" standing there. At age nine, I had another out-of-body experience, I believe, when I watched the doctors take out my appendix, though I was anesthetized at the time.

I've continued to have such experiences throughout my life. When, in the course of my studies, I went back to various periods of history and relived them, I was doing this by means of astral projection (or going out-of-body). The same was true when I "visited" and described the house of Joanne Foley's sister, when I was at Boston College—and the house was in California. I was astral-projecting, I believe, when I experienced and reported Roberto

Clemente's death while it was happening. The same is true when I relive cases for the police.

It may be, in fact, that many—if not most—of my predictions are made by brief, instantaneous astral projections. For instance, I may have astral-projected in the case of the man who'd been imprisoned, broken his arm, then shot himself and fell slumped forward. The same may be true in the case of the Akron, Ohio, woman who had part of her lung removed.

Many of the times I obtained detailed knowledge by psychic means can best be explained by astral projection. But even I am not sure of the exact mechanism at work.

However, I have had a number of experiences that cannot be explained in any other way than bilocation or astral projection. One of the most remarkable of these eventually led to my association with the American Society for Psychical Research.

It began modestly enough, in the elevator of the Brooklyn Heights hotel at which I was living in 1966, while teaching at St. John's University. I'd pressed the button for my floor and was waiting for the door to close when a woman I'd never seen before walked in. Without asking her which floor she wanted, I pressed the button for the tenth floor.

"How did you know which floor I wanted?" she asked, surprised.

"I have ESP," I told her flippantly.

She stared at me for a moment in surprise. Then she said, "You're just the person I've been looking for. I'm fascinated by that subject."

The woman, it turned out, was a New York psychologist. We got to talking and before long, she invited me to a dinner meeting of the Psychological Association, an organization for psychologists.

I attended that meeting, held in December 1966, as her guest. She'd invited me because she wanted some of her skeptical psychologist friends to meet me. Over dinner, she began to tell them of some of my paranormal experiences.

Sitting at our table, among others, was Dr. G., of a university on Long Island, and his wife. He listened to what Helen told everyone about me, smiling wryly. He obviously didn't believe in psychic phenomena or in my abilities.

"All right," he said finally, "I'll tell you what. I'll give you a date and you tell me what it means."

"Fine," I said, "I'll do my best." I knew he wanted me to read his mind, to tell him exactly what the date meant to him.

"The date is October 11," he said. He looked at me and smiled, waiting for my response.

"October 11?" I said. "It's the day before Columbus Day, but it doesn't mean anything to me outside of that." I turned to the others at the table. "Anyone else have a clue?" No one else did.

I leaned back in my chair and thought about it.

Suddenly, it came to me. "I know what you want. October 11—the Russian Revolution."

"What?" he said in surprise. "What's that you said?"

. As he spoke, the dinner table disappeared from my view. Instead, below me, as if I were dangling in mid-air, I saw the city of Leningrad, on October 11, 1917. I was hovering over a huge, beautiful gate in front of a palace. As I looked down, I described what I saw.

Off in the distance, a huge crowd of people—five thousand or more—were marching toward the gate, shouting angrily. They were stopped at the gate by the Czar's guards.

The group chose emissaries and they came forward. Members of the guard ran back to the palace. After a while—it seemed like forty-five minutes or so to me, though it took only a couple of minutes of actual time—the Czar came forth, apparently to treat with the emissaries. I described it all, as I watched.

As the Czar came forward, a body of soldiers formed up behind him unobtrusively. All eyes were on the Czar. Just before he would have reached the emissaries, he hurried quickly to the side. The troops opened fire on the protesters.

I saw it all. I saw men falling, blood pouring from their wounds. I saw others try to scramble onto a carriage and get away, when their horses were shot. I saw the panic in the faces of the protesters and the grim satisfaction of the Czar.

It was a scene of horrible carnage. Men, women, and animals were being killed by the hundreds. Even today, I remember it vividly. I wish I didn't.

Suddenly, I was back in Brooklyn Heights, at the dinner meeting. Dr. G., and the others were gazing at me in awe.

"Do you know what you described?" he asked.

"Not really—except that it was in Russia on October 11."

"You described the Czar's winter palace, the Hermitage, and its spectacular gate. Have you been there?"

"No, I've never been to Russia."

Dr. G. looked at me in astonishment. "Unless you saw it," he said, "you could never speak about it. Yet you described it in detail. The Hermitage, too. I know. I was there only a few months ago."

"Then I did read your mind," I said.

"No, I don't think so," he replied. "You saw things I never saw. You saw things no one could have seen unless he was there at the time."

"What was happening, what was going on with the Czar and the wage earners?"

"It was an historical event," he told me. "I don't remember all the details, but what happened was that a group of peasants—about five thousand of them—assembled outside the Czar's winter palace requesting an increase in wages. The Czar came out and promised to do something about it, then he quickly pulled to the side and his troops opened fire. About five hundred were killed, I believe."

I glanced around the table at the others. Their expressions showed their feelings clearly. They could scarcely believe what they'd heard.

"You're sure I wasn't just reading your mind?"

"That would have surprised me enough. But you described details I'd never heard. I'm not even sure there's a written record of everything you said."

Dr. G., who had spent three years in Russia doing research, knew of the incident I had described, but had never heard it told so extensively. He repeated to me that the only way I could have known such details was to be on the scene when the event occurred.

Which I was.

Dr. G. was now impressed enough by my abilities to invite me to lecture to his students at the university, which I did in January 1967.

Later, by the way, I did visit Leningrad. I saw the Hermitage and its marvelous gate. It was exactly what I had seen at the dinner table that night. I suppose I shouldn't have been surprised, but I was shocked. I stood in awe of the powers that had allowed me to see what had happened on that spot almost fifty years earlier.

As a result of my "trip" to Russia on October 11, 1917 (not the generally accepted date, by the way, but the correct one for the event I witnessed, according to the calendar then in use), I was introduced to Dr. Karlis Osis, director of the American Society for Psychical Research. I also met Marion Nestor, head of the ASPR's education department.

For the next three years, my contact with Dr. Osis and the ASPR was limited to an exchange of information. We discussed my psychic experiences and talked about what the ASPR was attempting to verify in its laboratory.

Then, in November 1968, I began serious work at the ASPR, undergoing a steadily increasing number of rigorous tests to determine my abilities and the extent of them. The results surprised even me.

One test involved a gadget called the ESPteacher—a little box with four or five buttons on it. I had to say which of these buttons would ring a bell. Electronic equipment constantly changed the circuitry, at random, so a different button was live each time—but which one?

I underwent several trials with the ESPteacher. On one occasion, I rang the bell nineteen times out of twenty-five attempts. On another, I managed the feat fourteen times out of twenty-five. The average person scores no better than chance on this machine, which means he rings the bell about four times out of twenty-five, on the average. On other trials, I rang the bell ten times out of twenty-five, then twelve times out of twenty-five.

I also did extremely well on another ESP test, something called the pendulum test. In the pendulum test, a pendulum is hung over a large sheet of paper divided into twenty-five squares. In advance of the test, the experimenters select a single square, mark their choice on a sheet of paper similar to the one under the pendulum, put it into an envelope, and carefully conceal the envelope.

Then the subject of the test is called in. It is his task to direct the pendulum to the square already selected by the experimenters. In a way it is a lot like dowsing—finding underground water with a forked stick or rod. I was the subject of this test on a number of occasions. According to Dr. Osis, my scores were extremely high:

"Dr. Tanous is one of the very few psychics or gifted men that we have in our laboratory and when he really gets down to work, it's phenomenal. In a series of tests given to him in the last eighteen months, his performance exceeded chance by three thousand to one."

My performance on these and many other tests was so impressive, I was told, that the ASPR wanted me to undergo far more elaborate testing. The objective was not to determine whether or not I had ESP. That was a settled issue. The American Society for Psychical Research wanted to determine whether or not I—or anyone else—could actually have an astral projection, a bilocation or an out-of-body experience.

Before long, Dr. Osis applied to the ASPR's board of directors for the additional funds needed to build the equipment that could perform a definitive series of tests on the out-of-body phenomena.

Meanwhile, I continued to have out-of-body experiences and bilocations outside of the lab. One day, in an elevator in the hotel at which I was staying, a man walked in and said, "Hi, Alex."

"Hi," I said.

"Do you remember me?" he asked.

"Well—to be perfectly honest, I don't think I do."

"I met you up at Liberty, New York," he said.

The more he said, the more confused I got.

"I want to tell you, you play a mean piano."

"I do? A piano?"

He looked at me curiously. "Aren't you Alex Tanous?"

"I am," I said. "But are you sure you haven't gotten me confused with someone else?"

"Of course I'm sure. I met you at a party up there. You were sitting at the piano, playing song after song. Everyone was crowded around you, singing. Don't you remember?"

"I've never been in Liberty, New York," I said.

"We got very friendly—you must remember me," he said.

But I didn't. And it wasn't a matter of poor memory. I never had been in Liberty, New York—still haven't, as a matter of fact. I'd never played a piano at a party. To tell the truth, I can't play well enough for that.

I'm convinced this is an example of bilocation. Somehow, without my knowledge, beyond my memory, some part of me had separated from myself and gone off. What's the explanation? I don't have any.

And maybe I'd be inclined to dismiss the incident as some kind of fluke, telling myself I'd been confused with someone else. Except that it happened again and again.

This time, I'll let a witness to the event describe it:

"My husband became ill in June 1969, and I was told by his doctors that his case was hopeless. His high blood pressure over the years had ruined his kidneys and it was only a matter of time. John was hospitalized February 9, 1970. I talked with Dr. Tanous and he made a note in his appointment book to go see him the next Monday at the hospital.

"When I went to the hospital Monday afternoon, my husband started talking excitedly about a man who had come in to see him that morning. He said the man had just spoken his name and then stood and stared at him. John was used to having a lot of different doctors come in to see him, but they had all asked him questions. This man did not say a word, except to call him by name. He described him and the description fitted Dr. Tanous perfectly.

"I did not see or hear from Dr. Tanous for several weeks and in the meantime, my husband passed away, February 24, 1970. The next Monday, Dr. Tanous called to say he had been away and inquired about John. I asked him if he had gone to see John. Dr. Tanous expressed his sympathy, and said he had seen him, saw there was no hope, but didn't know how he was going to be able to tell me.

"Then he told me the story. He had had to go out of town, and at the time he had promised to see John he was driving his car. He pulled to the side of the road and thought about him. He described the room, which bed my husband had been in, and the fact that the next bed had been empty. (This was something I had not known until I went to the hospital that afternoon, as the man who had been there went home that morning.) Then he described John, the way he was lying in bed, rather huddled up, and the puffiness in his face. He said he called him by name, he had answered 'yes,' stood there and looked [at] him, saw there was no hope, and left—which was the same way John had told it. Mrs. John P. McCartan, South Portland, Maine."

This was an unusual example of bilocation, in that I remembered the experience afterward. I had no memory of my bilocation to Liberty, New York. Nor do I have any memory of another bilocation. It is described below by E.A., of Tacoma, Washington, in a letter to a Maine friend, B.K. The letter was given to me by Miss K. It reads:

"Do I have a surprise for you. You may not recollect what you were doing the night of June 21 [1970] about 11:30 our time, but you and Dr. Tanous paid us a visit astrally in the mountains of Oregon. I asked someone how you were and he said, 'Speak to her yourself.' I could see you sitting on an empty garden chair across from me, with a man behind you (Dr. Tanous). He was slightly in the shadows. It was so tremendous—even the words and phrases were yours."

In this case, evidently, I brought someone along with me in my bilocation. How I did this, I do not know. I have absolutely no memory of the event, though I have no reason to doubt the letter writer, since it wasn't the first time such a thing had happened to me.

One of my friends, Arthur Ireland, of Wellesley, Massachusetts, has seen me bilocate several times. The first time was when he was in the hospital. He told me that I came to visit him there. I seemed as solid and real to him, he said, as though I was actually there—though I did not speak. I had been thinking about him at the time he said I visited him, but I made no attempt to bilocate. And I had no memory of the event. But I was able to describe everything about the hospital and his room, though I never saw it.

Another time, I appeared in his home, in his bedroom, on the window shade. It was in the middle of the night. His wife saw me first, awakened by my voice, calling her name. She woke up her husband.

"You really wanted to say something, you know," Arthur told me. "You were almost frightening. You wanted to tell me something, but weren't able to communicate. And there's no question, Al. I believe in God, but that was you. I know what you are and what you look like. You were trying to speak, but instead used your eyes."

Since then, I visited the Irelands several other times by bilocation, they report. "The first time," Arthur said, "I could just see your face. Each time after that I have been able to see more and more of your body."

Each time Arthur told me I had visited him in this manner, I could recall having thought about him or his wife. But I could not recall the visit.

It was about this time that the American Society for Psychical Research called me. They were ready to subject my out-of-body experiences to rigorous scientific study.

Intimations of Immortality

When I met Dr. Karlis Osis, back in 1967, I discovered we were both fascinated by one particular facet of the paranormal: apparitions at death.

Over the years, Dr. Osis had done a great deal of research on two types of death-related phenomena: the ghostly images, mists, clouds, etc., that doctors and nurses, among others, had reported seeing leave a person at the moment of his death; and the experiences of those who had "died" on the operating table or of heart attacks, only to be revived a few minutes later. Such people often told of feeling they'd "left their bodies" during the time they were "dead" and watched the scene as if they were observers.

I'd also been involved with both of these phenomena. As for out-of-body experiences, I'd had a number of my own, though I'd never been at the moment of death. And then there was my brother David's out-of-body experience, which he described to me in detail just before he died. After David's death in 1957, I joined the staff of Holy Ghost Hospital in Boston, a hospital for the incurable. My purpose in taking a job there was to observe people who were dying, to see if they had unusual experiences. On several occasions, I saw a shapeless mist drift away from a patient when he died.

Later, Dr. Osis and I discussed my experiences at great length. The ASPR, he told me, hoped soon to embark on a great project to determine whether or not something—anything—left the body at the instant of death. If such a thing actually happened—and it could be proved—it would be mankind's first scientific evidence that a soul exists, that at least in some sense, men are immortal.

The ASPR had long been interested in this question, but had not possessed the financial means necessary to investigate it scientifically. This was about to change, thanks to an Arizona prospector named James Kidd.

In 1946, Mr. Kidd wrote a will and placed it in a safety deposit box. A few years later, he disappeared without a trace. In 1964, his will was discovered, along with a list of the locations of large amounts of cash and securities.

His will said that his money was to be spent for "a research or some scientific proof of a soul of the human body which leaves at death." The Arizona courts decided that Mr. Kidd's will established a valid charitable trust and invited petitions from people and organizations who believed they were qualified to spend the money.

After examining more than one hundred claims, the money was awarded to Barrow Neurological Institute of Phoenix, Arizona. The Arizona Supreme Court, however, reversed this ruling, finding that the Institute "did not believe the soul could be a separate entity . . . which might survive the body's physical dissolution." And so the money—about $270,000—was awarded to the ASPR.

The ASPR put forth the hypothesis that "some part of the human personality indeed is capable of operating outside the living body (becoming ecsomatic) on rare occasions, and that it may continue to exist after the brain processes have ceased and the organism is decayed." It planned to test this hypothesis in several ways, one of which was to study the ecsomatic experiences—OBEs—of living persons.

Shortly after the courts awarded Mr. Kidd's money to the ASPR on December 29, 1972, Dr. Osis and his staff began a massive "talent search" for people who could have ecsomatic experiences at will. I was one of the more than one hundred who were contacted.

All of these people, myself included, agreed to participate in what the ASPR called a "fly in." At separate, given moments, each subject would attempt to leave his body and project himself in whatever way he could into Dr. Osis' office. In most cases, the distance involved was hundreds of miles.

When my turn came, I was in Portland, Maine. It was my task to "fly in" from there to Dr. Osis' office, look at the round coffee table there—which I'd seen many times—observe the objects that had been placed on the table, draw what I had seen, then, when the ASPR called later, describe my drawing over the telephone.

I underwent five separate trials. One time, I had the definite impression that something was wrong with the table. I saw an odd separation between various objects and colors. When Vera Feldman, an ASPR researcher, called me, I told her what I'd seen.

"That's amazing," she said. "The table was divided into two parts. We kept some objects on one side purposely. But what objects did you see?"

"Vera," I said, "I saw a candle. And something wrapped around it, like a ribbon. Also, there was a piece of wood."

"My God," she said.

On another occasion, I "flew in" and saw a basket of fruit. Vera called soon after.

"What did you see this time?"

"There was a basket of fruit on the table."

"Yes!" She said, "Yes!! That's what it was!"

On another occasion, I saw a knife lying on the table. It turned out to be a letter opener.

On yet another occasion, I saw Vera drinking a cup of tea. She later confirmed to me that she'd been drinking a cup of tea in Dr. Osis' office at the time.

And on my fifth trial, I once again saw Vera. This time, she bent over the table I was "looking" at. Again, she confirmed this by phone.

On each occasion, I viewed the table from my usual perspective—hovering above it, in mid-air. In fact, to check my pictures against what was on the table, ASPR researchers had to climb up on a ladder and look down.

This led to the most remarkable confirmation of all. At the appointed time, I "flew in" from Maine to Dr. Osis' office and observed the table from my usual hovering position. I didn't know it, but this time, the ASPR had brought in a psychic, Christine Whiting, to see if she could see someone in the room at the proper moment. I'd never met Miss Whiting.

This is what Dr. Osis later wrote of this trial:

"[On another occasion] we used human observers in the projection area. When a human observer was not especially psychic, he seemed to 'see' nothing. When an experienced psychic was in the projection area, she did see the projectionist at the approximate time of the projection.

"In one (case) a psychic from Maine felt that when he projected to the place of our stimulus display, he was bent over and floating over the display. The psychic who observed the area that evening did see someone hovering over the target display who was bent like a jackknife. This seemed a realistic observation. . . ."

Miss Whiting not only described my position and my location in space, she also saw me in a shirt with rolled up sleeves and in corduroy pants. I was wearing a shirt with rolled up sleeves at the time and I was wearing not corduroy pants, but pants with many thin stripes that even a short distance away look like corduroy.

Many people have asked me how I do this, what it feels like. Well, it doesn't seem difficult to do. I find myself a comfortable position in a quiet room, empty my mind of extraneous thoughts and say to myself, "Mind, leave my body now. Go to New York. Enter Dr. Osis' office" (for example).

Again and again, I repeat these phrases to myself, slowly, silently, thinking about nothing else. At a certain point, I find that I am without a body. I consist of a large spot of light, of consciousness, which gradually gets smaller and more concentrated.

Time then seems to stop for a moment and I am aware of an image. The image lasts for an indeterminate length of time, then disappears. Then I am conscious only of a spot of light. I have no other words to describe the experience. It is impossible to convey it in totality, I know.

After a while, quite automatically, quite beyond my control, I return. I would love to remain outside of my body, for it is very pleasant indeed, but I have no say in the matter. Before I can think about it, I am back, almost as if I have awoken.

I know it sounds simple—maybe too simple. When the procedure works, it is simple. When it doesn't, it's impossible.

I'm not always able to travel at will. Sometimes I take partial trips. It's as if my other self, the self I project, is inside an hourglass. On occasion, I am able to make all or most of my self—my consciousness—slip through the tiny hole in the middle all the way to the other side—the distant location. Other times, only a little bit gets through. Or none at all. I don't know why.

Then there's another problem. Very often, when I return to my body, I cannot remember where I've been. For this reason, I've taken to keeping a tape recorder running during my "travels" and describing aloud what I'm seeing. Otherwise, it might all be lost as soon as I come back, like a forgotten dream.

It took a long time, but the ASPR finally completed calculating the results of its talent hunt. I quote now from Dr. Osis' report on the outcome:

". . . We have by now tested about one hundred persons on long-distance OBEing. We tested the cream of the claimants. . . . In spite of careful selection, about 85 per cent of those who tried the experiment showed no awareness of the stimulus objects or persons in the target area, although generally they believed they had seen them. In most cases [they were] totally self-deceptive. . . .

"A significant but small number still remain where the OBE projection appears to be capable of perceiving (that is, the part of self projected can report on what it observed).

". . . Of those individuals in our studies who have shown some signs of OBE perceptual power, we did not find a single one who could see things clearly every time he felt he was out-of-the-body—the perception ranging from fairly good (i.e. clearly distinguishing some objects) to complete failure (i.e. producing very foggy or totally incorrect images)."

Eventually, others and I were invited to the American Society for Psychical Research to take part in more intensive OB experiments. While the equipment was being finished and installed, we did many informal tests—warm-ups, you might say.

One day, Dr. Osis asked me if I could take a trip out-of-body and locate Mary Lou Carlson, formerly a researcher at the ASPR, now living in California. "Well, I'll give it a try," I said.

I found myself a quiet room, got comfortable, closed my eyes and attempted to send myself to the West Coast—I didn't know exactly where. After a while, the images began to come to me. I described them aloud to Dr. Osis and the others, who were in the room listening.

"I see mountains and water," I said. "I see a house. But it's strange. It isn't a regular house. There's something odd about it."

"Yes," Dr. Osis said, excited, "tell us more."

I couldn't, not that day. But I went home that night and once again left my body, directing my other self toward Mary Lou Carlson's California home. This time, I saw the house clearly. Only it wasn't a house. It was a houseboat. I could see Mary Lou inside, puttering around.

The next day, I described it all to Dr. Osis. I was correct in many details. Mary Lou was living on a houseboat off the California coast, though there was no way I could have known this by ordinary means. Later, my description of the boat and of the clothing she was wearing when I "saw" her was also verified.

While at the ASPR, I demonstrated some of my other psychic abilities, in addition to my ability to have out-of-body experiences. I've already related one—finding that invoice lost in the filing system. A couple of instances involved psychometry, the ability to receive psychic images and or mental thoughts from an object.

One day, Bonnie Perskari handed me a woman's scarf.

"Can you tell me anything about the owner?" she asked.

I held the scarf in my hand and waited for the psychic impressions to come. "She's ill," I said. "She has to go to the hospital. I hope she does."

"You're right," Bonnie said. "That's it. She's sick and I've been urging her to go to the hospital for an operation for weeks."

Later, the owner of the scarf did go into the hospital and an operation corrected her problem.

Another time, Ann Johnson, another ASPR staff member, handed me a lighter. As I held it, the psychic impressions came through crisply and sharply. Most of us have words, and often, pictures flitting through our minds rather steadily. When I receive psychic impressions the sensation is no different—except that I somehow know the source is different, that the mental thoughts and/or images in my mind are not random, but significant.

In the case of the lighter, when I took it in hand, I had the immediate psychic impression of a hospital. And that's what I told Ann.

"The owner has just come out of the hospital. How did you know that?" she asked. "You couldn't have known that."

All I could do was smile and shrug. She was right. I couldn't have known. But I did.

In the course of my many readings and predictions, I've often relied on psychometry. After all, it was the first psychic skill I exhibited, when, at the age of eighteen months, I found "Mary Had a Little Lamb" among a stack of records, just by feeling their edges.

I've duplicated this feat several times as an adult, by the way. I was once at WPNO in Maine, talking with a disc jockey. I told him I would pick a record by a particular singer out of the many thousands they had on file, merely by touching record edges. And I did just that.

Another time, I was on WGAN "Maine Line" with Steve Morgan. He suggested we do ESP tests. He thought about a record and whispered what he was thinking to another announcer, Jack Tupper. I picked the record out of a stack on his desk. Next, they sent me out of the room, picked a record and announced their selection over the air. Then, after returning the record to the stack, they brought me back into the room. I reached into the stack and pulled out the record.

Over the years, I've done some quite remarkable things via psychometry. One instance was published in detail in the *Maine Sunday Telegram* on June 6, 1971. Reporter Paul Downing gave me a wrist watch to hold. Downing wrote in the *Telegram:*

> The man who had owned the watch was in his 80s and had been in gradually failing health for several years. He had a heart condition for which he took medication. He also had some of the usual infirmities of age, but he was not bedridden and was mentally alert. He experienced some hours of discomfort before his death, but finally fell asleep while sitting in his favorite reclining chair. He never woke up. The watch was on his wrist when he died (about two months ago).
>
> Holding the watch, Dr. Tanous said after a few moments: "There is one word that comes to me from this—and that is

illness. Secondly, the person is not a young person. I see a chair, it looks like a stuffed chair and this person is sitting in it.

"I don't know why, but this person looks unusual to me. The eyes—there's something about the eyes. In fact, the whole room, it's almost alive."

(It would seem that Tanous was tuned in on an impression from the man's last conscious hours as he sat in the chair, experiencing physical and emotional distress.)

"There will be sadness concerning this person. I don't know if this person is going into a very lingering illness and then death, but there is this type of sadness for the people around him. It may be going on now—I'm not sure. If it isn't, it will be."

He was asked to tell more about the chair.

"All that flashed to me was this—there's a big stuffed chair and this person is sitting in it. Just a quick flash—that is how these things come to me, in quick flashes. I saw the person in the chair and there was a cold chill over me. . . . There was something very sad at the end.

"This person used to be a very happy and jolly person, but the element didn't ring true here. There was something hanging when I saw this person, that he was not in the state that he usually is in. All I can get is that he's not himself—he's not himself. The face haunts me . . ."

(Comment: This is far too specific to be coincidence. Was it telepathy? [Did Tanous get this information from the reporter's mind?] If so, it would seem that telepathy would have revealed the one fact that Tanous had missed, and which was uppermost in the interviewer's mind—that the man was dead.)

The reporter's comment here is significant, I believe. I don't think I received this information from his mind, telepathically. I believe this was an out-of-body experience. Using the watch as a kind of psychic compass, I projected myself back to the owner's last hours. That's why I "saw" the chair so clearly. That's why my impression was not of death—which hadn't yet occurred—but illness. That's why I saw the man not being himself.

It may be—I cannot be certain—that most, if not all of my

psychometric experiences are actually out-of-body projections, in which I use the object as a guidepost or road sign. I believe this is what happened with the scarf and the lighter and it could even have happened with the record. In that case, all I had to do was project myself backward in time a minute or so and keep my eye on the record stack.

Of course, I have had many psychic experiences that can only be explained by telepathy. One of them was connected to the ASPR. It seems that they'd had a schedule change for their experiments and they wanted to tell me before I left Maine. But they couldn't get in touch with me by phone.

Bonnie Perskari and Ann Johnson decided to try to contact me telepathically. At three o'clock exactly on a Friday afternoon, they got together and projected, as strongly as they could, a message saying, "Alex, please call the lab as soon as you can."

At that moment, I was in Maine in my brother's law office, working on my income tax form. His secretary was typing it out for me. Suddenly, at exactly three I leaped up.

"I have to call the lab," I told the secretary.

"Couldn't it wait?" she asked. "It's three now and I have to leave at four. We'll never get this done if we interrupt things."

"Well," I said reluctantly, "all right."

Later, I visited the lab and told them of my impulse to call at three. That's when I learned of the psychic message they'd beamed at me. In my opinion, contact was definitely made.

The Search
for Scientific Proof

While all of this was going on, the ASPR was putting the finishing touches on four scientific devices that had been designed for use in the out-of-body experiments.

They are:

1. A semi-soundproof modified Faraday cage. Essentially, this is a big, light green steel box, about ten feet square. On the outside, it looks something like a commercial freezer. The entrance is through a massive steel door. Inside, the walls are covered with perforated white soundproofing tiles. There's a ventilation system, with an opening high on one wall, and a tangle of intercom wires in the middle of another. Some heavy carpeting covers the floor. The furnishing consists only of some large floor pillows and two wall lamps.

While it is not totally soundproofed, the steel box is a quiet, tranquil spot. There's a hush inside of it, something like the hush inside some telephone booths. The box is located in a small room, past an office, at the end of the hallway.

2. An "optical box." From the outside, this looks like a black plywood box perhaps three feet high and two feet wide with a round hole in the center—a window about three inches in diameter. Inside the box are two different systems. One is a flat wheel, divided into four quadrants. Each quadrant is painted a different color. This wheel is operated by a random number generator, an electronic device that insures there is no pattern whatever to the wheel's rota-

tion. The second device is based on a slide projector. The slide projector is set up with a number of pictures—usually five. It projects these pictures into a complicated system of lenses and mirrors.

When a person stands directly in front of the optical box and looks through the window, he sees what appears to be a picture superimposed over one of the color wheel's quadrants. And that quadrant might be occupied by any one of the four colors, depending on the wheel's position.

I say "appears'" because, in reality, no such superimposition exists. It's an optical illusion, created by the lenses and mirrors that catch and transfer the image produced by the slide projector.

Why the illusion of superimposition, rather than the reality? It's one of the many elaborate precautions the ASPR has designed into this experiment, to prevent the subject (enclosed in the steel box described above) from using any other psychic ability—clairvoyance, precognition, telepathy, etc.—to reveal what can be seen through the window.

For this reason, the equipment—not the experimenter—keeps an automatic record of what images have been offered. All ASPR personnel are kept out of the room with the optical box while experiments are in progress, to eliminate all chance of telepathic communication with the subject in the box.

In short, there is only one way for the subject to accurately know, at the moment of the experiment, what image is visible through the window: he—or some part of him—must be there.

If, under these conditions, any subject is able to say, with frequency consistently better than chance, what is visible in that hole, then the ASPR has hard evidence of the actuality of out-of-body travel.

3. A portable "optical box." This is a gadget designed for field use. It looks very much like a phonograph record—except that it's four inches thick. On one surface, a pie-wedge-shaped piece opens up to display a colored picture, which has been selected at random by a mechanism much like a roulette wheel. This is a precursor of the larger and more complex "optical box," which has replaced it in most experiments.

4. The "diving pool." Built originally for Robert Monroe, who

has written extensively of his own out-of-body experiences, this is a large opaque—in fact, copper-lined—plastic box about five feet long, three feet wide, and three feet high.

Inside the box are a number of small, very light objects, such as feathers. These are connected by wire to a Beckman "type RM" dynograph recorder. Also in the box, is a one-foot-square container of talcum powder with no top.

The optical box is designed to detect out-of-body *perceptions*, while the diving pool is intended to spot out-of-body psychokinesis or telekinesis. These words denote the ability to move an object without touching it, by mind power alone.

In experiences with the diving pool, subjects in the steel box are told to leave their bodies in their customary manner, project themselves into the diving pool and move one of the objects within it, or make some kind of mark—a foot print, a finger print, or even a simple "X" in the talcum powder.

If the subject succeeds in moving an object within the diving pool, the instruments will detect it. Why are instruments used? Why couldn't the diving pool be opened after an experiment and the objects be checked to see if they've been moved from their original positions?

Well, ASPR scientists believe that if a person can project some part of himself out of his body, that part—known among psychics as the "astral body"—might have very little physical power. It might be totally incapable of moving even a feather for any distance. But if the feather is suspended from a string, the astral body might be able to swing it a tiny fraction of an inch.

In addition to these major pieces of equipment, the ASPR also uses a battery of audio tape recorders to make an exact record of every word a subject says during an experiment, so there can be no doubt when results are calculated. Sometimes, I've brought my own tape recorder, in order to have my own record of what happened.

My work on this project has produced what Dr. Osis and the other ASPR scientists feel ranks with the most important results ever produced in the field of psychic experimentation. In its final, seven-hundred-page-plus report to the trustees of the Kidd estate, the ASPR said that my out-of-body experiments had substantially proved the original hypothesis—that there is something that can leave the body, some consciousness which "could be thought of as leaving the body at death."

I worked for two years with the out-of-body experiment. During this time I completed three series. According to Dr. Osis, the odds against my results being merely chance, as a whole, were a hundred to one.

In my first two series it was a learning process for me. By the time I was working with the third series, I had scientifically mastered the out-of-body travel. Further, I did it at will. In this third series the odds against its being merely chance were better than one thousand to one. According to the ASPR, my "scoring patterns [on the tests] were consistent with the OBE (out-of-body experience) hypothesis."

Furthermore, according to the ASPR, of all the psychics who took part in experiments in connection with the Kidd legacy, I was the only one who was actually able to provide substantial proof of the hypothesis.

For this reason, some have called me "the man who found the soul." I didn't find it, of course. It was always there. But my work has provided humanity with the first scientific evidence that the soul exists.

In the ASPR experiments, I have time and time again produced striking, inexplicable results—unless you accept the OBE explanation. I have seen the image in the optical box while enclosed in the steel box several rooms away. I have entered the diving pool and I have reason to believe that I've managed to swing the feather.

Because of the significance of these experiments, Dr. Osis has given me permission to describe in detail my own experiences while taking part in them, and to quote some of the comments he and other ASPR scientists have made to me in the course of these tests.

Let me start with some of the difficulties I've had with the equipment. In some ways, these difficulties are as significant as the actual results of the experiments. For example, in one trial, I curled up on the pillows inside the steel box and told my mind to leave my body, to travel to the optical box and look through the window.

I felt the familiar, drifting sensation. Light began to flit through my mind. All at once, I knew I'd done it—I'd left my body. I was "standing" in front of the optical box. But I couldn't see the image. Something was wrong.

"The light is too bright," I called into the intercom.

"No, it's not, Alex. The equipment is functioning perfectly. What do you see?" asked Bonnie Perskari, the researcher in charge.

"I can't see," I said. "The light is too bright. Something's wrong with the equipment."

Bonnie sighed. "All right. I'll check it out."

There was silence for a few moments. Then the door to the steel box swung open. Bonnie was standing there, a smile on her face. "You were right, Alex—absolutely right. It was a freak thing—the light illuminating the target was much brighter than it should have been."

I laughed. "How could I have known?"

"There's only one way," she said. "You must have been there. Too bad we won't be able to include this incident in our statistical analysis. Because of the malfunction, we're going to have to scrap the whole session entirely."

When I first began working with the optical box, I had another sort of difficulty altogether. I couldn't see the target image because I wasn't tall enough—at least my other self wasn't tall enough. The window on the front of the optical box is at about eye level for a person of medium height. My projected self, my astral body, as I see it, has hardly any height at all. It's a small ball of light. I couldn't see into the window unless I strained, unless I "stood on my tip toes"—and even then, I couldn't see well.

I explained my difficulties to Dr. Osis.

"All right," he said, "we'll build a platform for you."

He called in James Merewether, the ASPR's resident physicist, and Merewether built a small "porch" in front of the window—a little platform about two inches deep. It was exactly what I needed. From then on, my astral body, small as it was, was able to look into the window and report what was there.

After studying my test scores, ASPR researchers found they followed a pattern. Almost every time, I did very well in the first group of trials, then my performance tailed off. They felt it was a matter of challenge and interest. When the challenge was new and fresh to me, I did well. When it was old hat, I got bored.

There are two other possible explanations, I think. First, it may simply be that I get tired after a while. Out-of-body travel involves tremendous concentration, tremendous mental effort. It may be that

I can only do so much before I am exhausted. The second possible explanation: I am relaxed and loose at the beginning of a series of trials and I do well in that frame of mind. But as the day wears on, I try harder and harder. I press. I tighten up. And my test scores slip.

Frankly, I'm not sure why it happens. But it doesn't bother me. Dr. Osis and other ASPR researchers consider it just more evidence of my abilities. It's obvious, they say, that I am definitely able to do certain things on some occasions and not able to do them on others. "When he's wrong, he's dead wrong. But when he's right, he's dead right," Dr. Osis has said. If I had no ability, if I could not leave my body, the experiments would show no regular pattern. My errors and hits, over the long run, would be random. But they're not.

Just how often do I correctly report what can be seen through the window of the optical box? Let me quote from one of the tape recordings I made during and after the OBE sessions. Here is what an ASPR researcher told me:

"We did ten trials," she said. "On numbers four, five, and six, you got the colors all right in a row. The colors are very significant. You have hits on trials four, five, and six." (By "hits" she's referring to the subject, color, and position of the pictures.)

"Number one and number two are both partials." (This means I identified either the picture or its position on the color wheel, but not both.) "And both suggest the out-of-body. You also have some more isolated hits," (identifying picture, position, or color), "on trials nine and ten. But there's a whole cluster in the middle there."

To clarify, on these ten trials—my first of the day, naturally—the results were as follows:

TRIAL ONE: partial hit (picture, color, or position).

TRIAL TWO: partial hit (picture, color, or position).

TRIAL THREE: nothing.

TRIAL FOUR: color identified, picture and position identified.

TRIAL FIVE: color identified, picture and position identified.

TRIAL SIX: color identified, picture and position identified.

TRIAL SEVEN: picture and position identified.

TRIAL EIGHT: nothing.

TRIAL NINE: partial hit (picture, color, or position).

TRIAL TEN: partial hit (picture, color, or position).

As usual, I did less well on the second batch of ten and even more poorly after that. This is a typical example of my lab work at the ASPR. On some occasions, I fared much less well, my performance barely exceeding what would be expected by chance alone. Other times, however, I did even better. After one set of particularly good trials, Dr. Osis told me that my performance had exceeded chance by sixty-four hundred to one.

About this time, it was decided that I should attempt the diving pool, to see if, during an out-of-body experience, I could move an object within the sealed box.

Although Robert Monroe, the man for whom the experiment was designed, had never used the diving pool, others had. Most of them had reacted in the same way: they'd gotten sick. They'd had indigestion, exhaustion, or an attack of fainting. Why? Perhaps because the assigned task was so difficult.

That fact played a strange role in my best trial with the diving pool. When the experiment began, I took my place in the steel box, as usual, and the door was closed. Then I relaxed and began telling my mind to leave my body and head for the diving pool.

On the outside, Bonnie listened through the intercom, waiting for me to start talking, to start describing what I was doing. But I had nothing to say, for once. I was concentrating too hard on the task at hand.

"There was a long silence," Bonnie told me afterward, "and I got worried. I remembered what had happened with the others and I thought you'd also gotten sick. I was worried that you'd fainted or passed out and hit your head or something."

At any rate, after some minutes of total silence, Bonnie interrupted me. "Are you all right, Alex?" She called into the intercom.

"I'm fine," I told her. I said I'd been silent because I'd been concentrating on my job, because I was in some sort of altered state of consciousness. Though I was okay, Dr. Osis was disappointed. He'd been standing in the room adjacent to the diving pool, watching the Beckman recorder, waiting for the needles tracing out lines on the graph to show something unusual.

In the moments just before Bonnie had interrupted the experiment, one of the needles was beginning to register significant readings on the scale. "It was the kind of reading we were looking for," Bonnie later said.

Trying to salvage as much of the experiment as possible, Dr. Osis asked me what I'd been feeling at the moment of interruption. He said the needle had started moving up; then, when Bonnie and I started talking, it fell back.

"I was moving it," I said. "I just know I was. I could feel it move."

The brief instrument readings were not conclusive. One reason: the tests are conducted at ASPR's headquarters in midtown Manhattan, where electrical interference is commonplace, as are rumbling trucks, even flushing toilets in floors directly above or below the laboratory. Any one of those things can upset the delicate instruments. ASPR scientists are constantly trying to refine their readings, to exclude any spurious signals.

Someday, the equipment may be sufficiently refined that ASPR researchers can go back to that experiment and others in which I participated and determine conclusively if there was actual movement in the diving pool. Until then, though, all that can be said is that the results are very, very interesting.

I did participate in another experiment in which scientific instruments showed beyond a reasonable doubt that I had left my body. Because the results were so definitive, it's worth describing at length.

In the early months of 1974, Dr. Osis and I talked at length about my impression that during my out-of-body experiences, I see myself as a tiny ball of light. Would it be possible, we both wondered, to detect this ball of light in the target area? From previous experiments, we knew my presence could not normally be detected during out-of-body experiments by human observers (though there was that remarkable exception during the fly-in tests). Could an instrument detect and record this light, we wondered.

To find out, we made arrangements to use the facilities of the Energy Research Group, a part of the Institute for Bioenergetic Analysis, on Grand Street in New York City. This organization is composed of a number of biochemists, physicists, and other scientists. They're attempting—among other things—to study psychic phenomena on the basis of the electromagnetic energy involved, if any.

One of their projects is an experiment designed to see if scientific instruments can record a person's aura. Here are some extracts from their first preliminary report on this work:

"Many observers have reported seeing an envelope of radiation or field surrounding living organisms. In order to determine whether any of these radiations are measurable by currently available instruments, a comprehensive evaluation of promising methods of detection was undertaken. As a result of this study, it was decided to use a highly sensitive photomultiplier tube as standing the best chance of detecting this radiation.

"A photomultiplier is a device which responds to extremely small quantities of light, by producing a measurable amount of electrical charge. . . . A tube was utilized which responds to light in the visible and ultraviolet, but not in the infrared. (This) ruled out heat effects; the very high sensitivity in the visible and ultraviolet allowed the examination of the color spectrum reported by many observers.

"Our program was to use this photomultiplier tube to quantitatively analyze the intensity, the optical frequency spectrum (color range), time dependence (pulsation rate), and spatial distribution (shape) . . .

"Utilizing this method, we have been able to measure the light output of an experimental subject. The level of this light is exceptionally low and is in the range of 10 to 50 photons per second, as recorded at the photocathode. This represents an average signal of approximately 20 per cent above the background noise. . . .

"However, in some individual interaction periods, the subject is able to give an increased signal as high as several hundred per cent above the background noise. Each series of measurements was preceded and followed by measurements of background noise (static). These indicated stability . . . so that the increases of the signal with the subject present are statistically significant. In addition, the increases in the signal coincide with the subject's attempts to increase his energy field and his verbal descriptions of his perception of these increases. . . .

"Nearly all individuals were able to produce a signal from the photomultiplier tube. Others . . . were unable to effect . . . it. The experimental subject has to voluntarily increase his field in order to achieve maximum signal. He does this by deep breathing and by small vibratory movements of his body. When the . . . control subjects use the same . . . techniques, there is no increase in signal. Thus, not only infrared, but also movement, vibrations, static charge, and skin fluorescence (subjects are tested when nude) are ruled out as causes for the experimental subject's signal increase. . . .

"(We also found) that different inanimate objects with similar emissivity (to) human skin and heated to varying temperatures from 30° C. to 90° C. do not increase the phototube output. This rules out radiant heating of the phototube cathode, as well as infrared, as a source of the increased signal when the subject is present.

"The work done to date indicates strongly that a human being radiates a field that can be detected by a phototube. Our knowledge of the properties of this field needs to be expanded further. . . ."

When Dr. Osis and I went to the Energy Research Group, along with other ASPR personnel, we found they were eager to set up an experiment to detect my out-of-body presence in the target area, if indeed, it could be detected.

Normally, the subject of aura experiments sits inside a large, opaque black box, nude, while the photomultiplier attempts to pick up any light his body radiates. In the experiment designed for me, several objects were placed inside that box. I was stationed in another room—the john—which was a considerable distance from the box.

During the experiment, I was supposed to project myself out-of-body into the opaque black box. While there, it was my job to look around, attempt to identify the objects left for me to see. Meanwhile, the photomultiplier tube would be turned on, to detect my light energy, if any.

Now I knew there was a chair inside the box. Subjects of the aura test sat on it. But I had no idea what other objects had been placed in the box, or where.

When the experiment started, I turned on my tape recorder and left it running. I often forget what I've seen or said during an out-of-body test. This time, I wanted to be sure to have a permanent record of my words.

And here are excerpts from the transcript of that tape:

"I am sitting in the john, in a sort of a director's chair, and I'm to astral project into a very dark room, which I have seen. I will now breathe quite heavily and go into certain exercises. I'm going to just slump into the chair, kind of, put my feet against the wall . . . and just see what happens. I'm having a little trouble getting into the out-of-body . . . (silence and jet noise).

"A ball of light is beginning to appear in my mind. I'm projecting myself now . . . I seem to be in front of two lights. I'm trying to come down to hit the target on the chair. One of the targets is on the chair, the other one is not. One of the targets is on the floor and it's square to me. I'm touching something. It's as if it were soft, like leather. The object on the chair is hard. It's circular, clear or white. . . .

"I am now over the chair. I am now seeing this circular thing on the chair. I'm hovering. (Silence.) I am now coming down on the chair. I am down. My light is getting smaller. The target on the floor seems to be closer to the wall, the left side. It's square, it's soft. I seem to be rising now.

"Come on, let's go touch, let's go touch the object on the chair, touch the object on the chair. There you go, touching it, touching . . . it looks like a circular raised thing, leaning against the back of the chair.

"Pow! There's a burst of light. The object on the floor feels like it's a wallet. The one on the chair is tall, circular—by circular, meaning it appears circular as if it were a statue. . . . (long silence)

"This time I see bright lights shining, pretty bright lights, with lines running across. A POW of explosion—white! I'm dangling, dangling, dangling. Come on . . ."

And then I was back, all together again. The experiment was over. I opened the door and came out into the light, blinking, holding my tape recorder (which was still running, by the way).

I began talking about what I'd experienced with Bonnie Perskari.

"The objects," I began, "all right, one was on the floor, to the left, square. The one on the chair had a form, it appeared as a shape to me."

"You mean the target?" Bonnie asked.

"Yes. I thought at first it was a tube . . . then, suddenly, I found myself with a burst of light. Then I started to hover from the chair down to the floor on the left and I saw this square thing and it felt like leather or something. That's all I seem to remember. The tall shape—and that soft square," I said.

"The shape on the chair, was it a tall object?" Bonnie asked.

"Well, it appeared that way to me. . . . How long was I out, Bonnie?"

"Twenty-one minutes."

"Twenty-one minutes! I didn't realize it was that long."

Bonnie, Jim Merewether and Dr. Karlis Osis, from the society, and Carl Kirsh, M.D., and Ted Wolfe, from the New York Medical Center, along with Bob Whipple, stood by while the door to the box was opened.

Leaning against the back of the chair was the heating element from a coffeepot, circular at the bottom, tall, tubular, hard—exactly as I'd described it. It was silver-colored and I'd said it was clear or white. Also on the chair was a scissors, which I hadn't seen at all, for some reason.

"Here," Ted Wolfe said, "put your hand down on the floor and you will feel the thing you felt during the experiment. It's a rubber pad. It wasn't meant to be a target object, but it's in here, that's for sure. It was exactly as you described it."

When I put my hand on the rubber pad, I could hardly believe it. About ten minutes earlier, while sitting in the john, I'd felt the same object psychically. The sensation was absolutely identical.

"What about the instruments? Did they show anything?" I was naturally very anxious to know whether or not the photomultiplier had registered anything while I was out-of-body.

Ted Wolfe told me the instruments had recorded three distinct peaks of light, each well above the background noise. "The photomultiplier acted as though it had a subject in front of it," he said. "It's the sort of reaction we get when we have a person in the box."

The next day, Bonnie Perskari wrote a report of the incident for Dr. Osis and ASPR records. She found that at almost the exact instant I saw those bright lights, the photomultiplier registered light in the room.

While I was taping my words, Bonnie was taping what was being said by those watching the photomultiplier. In her report, she compared the two tapes. During the twelfth minute of the experiment, I began talking about "bright lights shining. . . ."

At almost the same moment, Dr. Wolfe was saying, "It passed the target level! It jumped quite a bit from the eleventh (minute)." (That was the first time it went above the empty room level.)

"If you listen to the tape," Bonnie wrote, "you will hear that Al sounds surprised and awed when he speaks of the lights, etc. . . . The twelfth minute was not the peak (that was the fourteenth minute), but it was the first strong sign of something happening, both on the chart and with Al Tanous.

"So far, I would say it looks very good."

I underwent several more trials that day, without further result—which is not surprising, in view of my pattern. But nobody, especially myself, was very disappointed. What I'd done was so remarkable, so significant, that its importance was obvious to everyone.

Since the experiments at the Energy Research Group, I've undergone a good deal of additional testing at the ASPR. In one group of tests, I underwent out-of-body tests while connected to EEG equipment that read my brain waves. The question: did the electrical activity in my brain change when I was out-of-body?

The results of this test were inconclusive. There were some slight changes in the electrical activity in my brain, but they weren't always co-ordinated with my test results. Dr. Osis believes there are definite changes, but that the EEG is not sensitive enough to detect them. "It's like trying to take your temperature by laying a thermometer on your arm," he says. The EEG, he notes, can detect gross changes—when several million brain neurons shift gears. But when the change involves only a few hundred thousand, the EEG is helpless.

Another group of tests has produced highly significant results, however. In these, I've been able to do something no other psychic, no other out-of-body subject has done: I've looked at my identifications and designated *which were accurate and which were not*, by remembering how I felt during the experiment—whether or not I felt complete, partial, or no separation at all. These designations have been remarkably correct. As a result, I've had further confirmation of my out-of-body experiences.

I've often wondered why I do so well in laboratory tests, while many other psychics do so poorly. I've heard several complain they couldn't function in the laboratory, that it was cold and forbidding. They would much rather perform their feats in front of audiences. Some say they need audiences or they can't produce psychic phenomena.

I don't feel that way. I don't particularly love machines and measuring equipment, but the ASPR is an organization of people—warm, likable, sympathetic human beings—rather than a laboratory, so far as I am concerned. The people at the ASPR are among my favorite people.

I enjoy working with them. I like the challenge they offer. I have fun doing the experiments. To tell the truth, I wouldn't mind moving in. But I have another motive beyond personal enjoyment. My lab work offers me the opportunity to share my knowledge and abilities with others. And I am obligated to do this, I believe, since I have been given this gift.

I think a few words about the content of these laboratory experiences are in order here. I am completely aware of how impossible it seems to the average person that anyone can leave his body, observe something, then return—without ever having moved physically. If I hadn't done it myself, I too would find it hard to believe. But it is possible, and the ASPR has established this with rigorous scientific accuracy.

The ASPR's work and mine won't convince everyone, I know. I've found that people tend to reject out-of-hand any phenomena that threaten their view of the world, whether this view is highly scientific and very logical, or highly religious and based on the deepest sort of faith.

Most people would sooner deny the phenomena—no matter how well documented, no matter how scientifically controlled and observed—than change their own world views. And this is understandable. A person's perception of the world is at the core of his beliefs. When it is challenged, all of his other beliefs are also challenged, if only indirectly. Some of these beliefs are dearly held indeed.

For those of you who would deny, I urge an open mind. Consider the evidence I have related here (and other evidence you may come across) as objectively as possible. Use truth as your only basis for acceptance or rejection.

If you do this, you may be forced to change your mind about many things. But your world view will be more accurate for the change, and your peace of mind on a more solid footing.

And remember the deeper significance of out-of-body experiences. They may be the first piece of scientific evidence in the immortality puzzle.

My out-of-body experiences have brought me closer to my religious beliefs. I have the feeling that I have shared in something divine. When I go out-of-body, I see lights and beauty. Sometimes, I don't want to come back. But I know I have to. I know that unless I return and share this gift with others, I would never be happy.

Ghosts and Spirits
I Have Known

Out-of-body experiences may give us the first glimmerings of scientific proof of immortality. But I've already had quite a bit of not-so-scientific evidence.

I have, on several occasions, made contact with ghosts and spirits.

I am not a medium—at least not a classic medium, the sort who holds seances, goes into trances, etc. As far as spiritualism, mysticism, and the occult are concerned, I'm a skeptic. I feel the same way about possession by spirits and exorcisms.

On the other hand, I have been able to communicate with spirits, or at least to get in touch with their energy, on a psychic level. This makes me what's called a "conscious medium." I believe I've had this ability since childhood, when I had spirit playmates. There is no question in my mind that these playmates were deceased relatives. My family was able to identify them.

As I grew older, however, I lost the ability to see my spirit playmates. So it must be for many children. I think children have the ability to break through the barriers of time and space and contact people from either the past or the future—other children, most likely, since children tend to gravitate toward one another. But this ability vanishes after repeated challenges from the parental view of reality.

It was not until many years after these childhood experiences that I again felt comfortable enough with my psychic self that I had the freedom to contact spirits.

Several striking instances took place during one of my several trips to Europe. On one of these, I traveled to Leysin, Switzerland, to visit a niece who was spending the summer there attending school.

Leysin is a small town reached by a cog railway, surrounded by craggy mountain peaks. If the scene sounds like Thomas Mann's *The Magic Mountain*, it's with good reason. The college my niece was attending was once a tuberculosis sanitarium.

When I arrived in Leysin, my niece, Mary Ellen Tanous, wasted no time introducing her "psychic uncle" to her girl friends. And before long, the conversation turned—as it so often does when I'm around—to matters psychic.

My niece's friends told me they had a problem in this area. Every night, when all of them were in bed, they heard the sounds of heavy breathing and footsteps coming from a room on the floor above them, the fourth floor. The problem: the fourth floor was totally unoccupied.

Now it was true that those rooms had known the sound of labored breathing in the old days, when weakened lungs struggled to capture oxygen from the thin mountain air. But that was decades ago.

I visited the room on the fourth floor that the girls believed the sounds were coming from. Then I climbed to the top floor, the sixth, and out onto a balcony commanding a magnificent view of mountains and valleys.

Then, I opened myself up to whatever psychic impressions might come. I felt a chill come over me. Then I began to relive events from the past. I saw an old woman, a very wealthy woman, being dragged, protesting, to the balcony, then thrown off. The murderer, I sensed, was one of her relatives, someone who couldn't wait until she had died to inherit her wealth. Her room was on the fourth floor.

The breathing the girls had heard was this woman's breathing. The loud footsteps were those of the woman and her murderer, on the night of the crime. I had the psychic impression that the spirit of the woman was lingering about the building, causing these noises, with the hope that the true nature of her death would be discovered. At the time the spirit somehow communicated to me, her death was thought a suicide.

I told the girls what I had discovered and thought nothing more of it. I never dreamed I'd have any confirmation of my spirit contact. But I did get it, and in a rather strange way.

I was lecturing on ESP and psychic phenomena to a group of American teachers at the college at Leysin. After I told this story, one of them came up to me and said the story reminded her of a book she'd read, *The Rack*, by A. E. Ellis. At the time, I thought nothing of it. I could easily imagine a novelist inventing such a plot. Still, I mentioned it in a press interview when I got back to the United States.

Later, someone who'd read that interview sent me a copy of the book. It turned out to be nonfiction. It described, among other things, the same incident I had described, detail for detail—except that it labeled the woman's death a suicide. It seems she'd been found dead beneath the balcony in the snow. The place? The sanitarium in Leysin, Switzerland.

What's the explanation? I don't know. The incident seems too remarkable to be described as a coincidence, even if it were the only time such a thing had happened to me, which it wasn't, not by a long shot.

In 1973, when I visited London, I happened to go to the famous Westminster Abbey. Once more, I felt a chill come over me. Suddenly inexplicably, I felt I was in touch with the spirit of Elizabeth Barrett Browning. I stood still for a while and let the spirit touch me. Then I walked over to where Robert Browning had been buried. (Westminster Abbey is filled with such graves. The stones that make up the floor are their tombstones, and their names are carved into them.) Standing over Browning's grave, I felt his wife's spirit was with him. I found I had the irresistible urge to speak.

I was with friends at the time, who saw the troubled expression on my face. "What's wrong?" asked one.

"I have to say something," I said. "I love thee with the breath, smiles, tears, of all my life!—and, if God choose, I shall but love thee better after death."

One of my friends looked at me in surprise. "Do you know what you just quoted?" she asked.

"Not exactly," I said. "I don't even remember what I said. I just felt I wanted to say it."

"You were quoting Elizabeth Barrett Browning's poem, the one that begins, 'How do I love thee? Let me count the ways. . . .'"

"But I don't know how it goes," I protested.

"Well, you quoted the last line word for word. She wrote it for her husband, you know. She wrote it for Robert Browning."

I looked down at the floor. The stone I was standing on had Robert Browning's name carved into it.

In August 1973, I found myself employed as a ghostly messenger service for other spirits. I had flown to Decatur, Alabama, to meet with a friend. When I arrived, a young woman in his office asked me for a reading.

"Write down your questions," I said, "and while you're writing, I'll go to the bathroom."

I walked up the hall, entered the bathroom, and closed the door. Suddenly, I felt a chill—and a definite psychic image entered my mind. I had the mental picture of a beautiful lady with a dark cloud over her head. The lady spoke to me. I heard her words not through my ears, but in my "mind's ear."

"I want you to tell my daughter there are some papers in my house on an antique shelf—" As she talked, an image of the shelf flashed into my mind. "These papers must be taken care of. You tell my daughter about these papers."

I unlocked the door and returned to my seat.

"I haven't finished writing out my questions yet," the young woman said.

"That's all right. I have something to tell you."

I told her about my psychic image, describing the woman in detail.

"That's my mother," she said, almost overcome by shock. "You've described her perfectly. She died recently, you know."

"No," I said, "I didn't know. I'm sorry to hear it."

She nodded.

"Tell me," I said, "do you have an antique shelf in your home?"

"Why, yes," she said. "Why do you ask?"

"Your mother told me there were some important papers on that shelf, papers that must be taken care of."

"I don't think so," she said. "I don't know of any papers. But I'll ask my father. He's still living there."

Later, she called me. She and her father had searched the shelf, which was more like a bookcase. On the top, forgotten and neglected, were all the unanswered letters and sympathy notes her mother had received during her long illness.

Another time, a woman came to me and asked me for a reading. Her husband had died recently and she was hoping I could tell her where he put his will. Even before she sat down, I got a psychic message.

"Do you know someone named Ina?" I said.

"No, I don't. My husband's name was Ira, though."

"I have a message for you," I said. "The will you're looking for is in your house"—and I told her the exact location.

Then, we did the reading, in which I told her many things about herself and her family and advised her on what course of action to follow in the future. As she was about to leave, her face suddenly turned pale. She screamed—"Ina, Ina!"

"What's the matter?" I asked.

"Our daughter called her daddy, 'Ina,' when she was a child, when she couldn't pronounce 'Ira.' "

Shaken, she left and went home immediately to look in her house in the spot I had suggested she might find the will. She called soon afterward. It was exactly where I said it would be.

What's the explanation? I don't know. But I don't think it's coincidence.

After I began participating regularly in ASPR experiments, I found myself with many new opportunities to make spirit contacts. People often call the ASPR when strange things happen in their homes—the appearance of a poltergeist, for example. A poltergeist is a mischievous entity who makes noises, throws objects about, causes fires, and breaks domestic crockery. On request, and when the phenomena observed are particularly interesting, the ASPR sends a team of researchers to investigate. In the last couple of years, I've been a member of that team on several occasions.

One time, the ASPR was asked to investigate one side of a two-family house in Brooklyn. The occupants had reported poltergeist activity. When Dr. Osis and I came to visit, we saw nothing odd.

The only sounds were some pet birds in a cage. They were making an awful racket.

Then that familiar cold feeling came over me. I knew I was in the presence of spirit energy. Suddenly, the birds stopped chirping, lapsing into total silence. I started up the stairs.

As I walked up toward the second floor, Dr. Osis standing below me, watching, I began to receive a flood of psychic impressions. I began to get a sense of how the house had looked before it was divided in half. I saw how the furniture had been arranged. Then I started to pick up the spirit of a woman.

I saw her, pale and translucent, standing at the top of the stairs. Then, slowly, an image began to form beside her—a man. She seemed to notice his appearance at the same time I did and she pushed him behind her, annoyed. I described what I saw to Dr. Osis.

Then, I attempted to make contact. "You don't want to talk to me?" I heard myself say.

"Ask her why, ask her why," Dr. Osis urged.

I did just that.

Her words echoed in my mind. "Well, you wouldn't understand." She had a distinct Italian accent.

"What wouldn't I understand? Why are you here, why have you been making such a fuss?"

There was anger in her eyes. "You wouldn't understand," she repeated. "It could have been better, it should have been better."

"What could have been better?"

"The way it ended," she said bitterly.

Try as I might, I could get her to say no more. I started down the stairs, finally.

"You may return, if you wish," she told me.

"I will," I said. "I'll be back very soon."

Dr. Osis and I then talked to the present occupants of the house. I described the woman I had seen and her manner of talking. The ghostly figure was a perfect match for the house's previous occupant, who, with her husband, had originally come from Italy. The man I'd seen looked—in every detail—like her husband. And I soon discovered why she'd pushed him behind her: he was still alive.

Two weeks later, I returned to the house in Brooklyn, along with Dr. E. Haraldsson of Iceland, who was with the ASPR at the time. This time, it was very hard for me to get into contact with the woman, but finally, she appeared.

She was different this time, even less substantial than before. And when she walked, she seemed to wobble, as if something were wrong with her leg.

"I must go," she said. "I must go."

"Why?"

"It wouldn't do any good to tell you what happened. My protests are useless."

"Wait—wait," I said. "Before you go, I need some kind of evidence that I have talked to you."

She hesitated, extremely reluctant to comply. "What do you want?" she asked.

"A word, a noise, something that can be picked up by the tape recorder."

She seemed to sigh. Then I heard it, a sound like two pieces of metal being banged together. When the sound stopped, she was gone.

What do I make of this? I do not know.

On another occasion, I visited an apartment in Queens with members of the ASPR staff. The occupants had gotten in touch with the ASPR because they were having poltergeist problems—blankets flying, paper ripped, etc.

I slowly walked through the apartment. When I got to the master bedroom, I paused. I sensed energy present. And there on the bedroom wall appeared the image of a beautiful young woman with lovely long hair. She was in her early twenties. Next to her was an old man, head bowed. An expression of—I know no other way to describe it—thirst on his face. As I watched, the young woman slowly aged, eventually ending up as an old lady. It was as if she were demonstrating to me how she had looked at various periods of her life. The old man did not change during this demonstration. He continued to suffer. Then the old lady became a young woman again. Throughout it all, I heard no words, only messages in my mind. Finally, the picture on the bedroom wall vanished. I returned to the living room to talk to the occupants of the apartment.

The apartment was occupied by a man, his wife, and their three children. When I described the man and woman I had seen, it meant little to them. Then, the wife's mother returned from a European trip and I returned to the apartment and told her what I had seen.

She listened with astonishment. Evidently, I was describing—in extraordinary detail—her own mother and father. Her father had died in a fire in his native Latvia.

On the second visit, I went back into the bedroom. I tried to call forth the spirit again, and, after a while, the woman's image reappeared on the wall, briefly old, then young. I tried to speak to her with my mind, asking her for a sign of identification.

Perturbed, she began speaking to me in a foreign language—most of which I heard as English. I remembered only one foreign phrase.

I walked back into the living room and repeated what I had heard to the lady who'd just returned from Europe—the ghost's daughter. She turned bright red, remembering the phrase as one of her mother's favorites, applied to anyone who perturbed her. She was somewhat embarrassed. It seems that her departed mother had heaped some salty Latvian curse words on my head.

Once more, I went into the bedroom, to confront the lady on the wall. "I can't help you if you don't tell me what's bothering you," I said.

"They didn't keep their promise," I heard her say, in my mind.

"What promise?"

"They promised they were going to name my great-grandchildren after my husband and me, but they didn't."

"Would it satisfy you if they had the names changed?" I asked.

But I got no answer. The image faded away.

I told the family what she had said, and they made the change she'd requested. After that, the poltergeist disturbances ceased.

My strangest experience with a ghost or spirit occurred last year, at the Dandy homestead in upstate New York, where I had gone, along with Father Alphonsus Trabold of St. Bonaventure University and a New York University film crew, to investigate a report of poltergeists.

"The disturbances began on June 29, 1970," according to the house's owner. "We had noise without action. A window slamming

—when it didn't slam. We had things falling when they really didn't fall. Then we had action without noise. A lamp breaking—and we didn't hear anything. Some kind of a furry creature jumped on Beth (a young girl who lived in the house). I knew it was not one of our animals. I had them downstairs. I think that was what frightened me most."

I went into the house with the film crew, Father Trabold beside me. Our goal was to rid the house of its poltergeist, if possible. It wasn't long before I felt spirits there—many of them, for the house was more than a hundred years old. The tape recorder picked up my words. Here are some exerpts from the recording:

"Birds quiet. A girl lying in bed, calling for help, getting no response from her mother and father, who are arguing. I am now in a very dead cold. The chill is getting even stronger. . . . The birds will remain quiet as I leave and draw the energy from the room. . . .

"There are other energies in the room which are also affecting me. . . . The vibrations are those of a very elderly lonely woman, in her nineties. The energies are of certain things that have disquieted her over the years. . . .

"The other energy is of a girl—oh, I would say twelve or thirteen —who was raped and killed. The young girl was raped by a man who was a bachelor and the most incredible thing about it all was that he hated women very much. . . .

"Again, the chills are hitting me. . . . I'm picking up a young man, eighteen or nineteen, who was killed in an accident. . . . For some reason, all these energies are converging here.

"There's also been the death of a man in this room, a death which was a drastic death of agony—not a murder or suicide. What I am now going to do is pick up this energy. . . .

"All right, the energy has now been picked up. As you see, the lights go out. The energy force is forcing me to say that it does not want to leave. The energy is here . . . but her financé had a very tragic death. The energies are sorrow energies. Tragic. The person —the man—drowned and the woman has never gotten over it. The woman locked herself in this room from time to time and would not come out at all. . . .

"You must, you must, you must—time has gone, a child cannot be born. I am going to force you, force you. You must leave. The answer is: no, you cannot stay. You can't stay. (Heavy breathing, gasping.) All right, all right, let's go. Let's go. All right.

"The burn is there. I know you burned me. I realize it. But I'm going to take you with me, no matter what happens. I'm holding onto you. Go ahead. No, you're not. You're not going to take over. I'm going to have you. All right, going? Let's go, let's go. I want to break you, break you. (Gasping.)"

Later, Father Trabold described what I'd been through, from his point of view:

"You were first speaking in the same tone, in the same way, in a very calm way, and sort of commenting on the different vibrations you got. And then all at once you stopped for a moment, and then —you were completely unaware of us—you started talking to the entity that was there—a young blind girl. And it was very evident that this spirit did not want to leave. You were saying with more force each time that it should leave and then as you did this, your body began to contort, especially your face, your hands. Your fingers curled up and your arms began to tense up, your mouth began to open and contort. . . .

"You began to sway and to start to fall backward and I put my arm around you and began to hold you . . . the weight was almost more than I could hold. . . . Whatever it was was putting up a tremendous battle . . . but you didn't give up."

As for me, I was just glad it was over. I felt as though I'd been through a horrible struggle. I'd won, all right, but not by much. And then there was the burn. I'd felt as if the entity had burned me during our battle.

I unbuttoned my shirt and looked at my side, where I'd felt the burn. There was a patch of raw skin, about the size and shape of a fifty-cent piece. It was badly burned, as if it had been exposed to the summer sun for many hours with no protection.

I felt I was lucky to escape with no more damage than that.

After my attempt to "depsych" the Dandy house, Father Trabold performed an exorcism. Evidently, our combined efforts were good enough. From that day on, things have been normal at the Dandy house.

Out of This World

At least five times in my life, I have had some kind of contact with creatures I can only describe as from another world. Most of these contacts have been brief, indirect, even accidental. At least one, however, was face-to-face.

My first contact—and it was only a psychic contact—came at a completely unexpected moment. I'd been called in by a family to help locate their missing child. The circumstances of the disappearance—if one is to believe the parents—were strange indeed. The child, a preschooler, had been playing in the back yard, in full view of the mother, who was making dinner in the kitchen. She turned away from her work for only an instant—to get something out of a cabinet, she said. When she turned back, her little boy had vanished.

There was the usual extensive search, but he was never found. Police were puzzled, because the back yard of the house was well protected from the street. It was hard to imagine a stranger finding his way back there, especially without being noticed. Further, the yard was huge. It was surrounded by thick woods, but it would have taken the little boy some time to walk to the trees. The last time the mother had seen the boy, he was playing in his sandbox, which was virtually in the dead center of the yard.

Nevertheless, police and Boy Scouts combed the surroundings. They covered every square foot of woods for half a mile around.

(Past that, there was a housing development.) There were a few small ponds and these were carefully dragged.

When I was called in, after about two weeks, I walked the area myself, trying to sense vibrations. But I couldn't pick up anything out of the ordinary. I went home and thought about it. There was only one way I could get a clue to the boy's whereabouts, I realized: astral projection. So I settled myself into my most comfortable chair, closed my eyes, and asked my mind to drift away, to seek out the little boy.

The visions that came into my mind as a result of that out-of-body trip were among the strangest I have ever experienced. I could see the boy—alive and well. But the environment was totally unfamiliar. Even now, I have no words to describe it. He was in another place (if place is the right word). He had no tangible location in regard to the real world.

The boy seemed surrounded and supported by a bizarre kind of energy, as though he were elsewhere in time and space. I'm sorry I cannot describe it any better than that. I felt as though he'd slipped through the real world somehow and disappeared, much as planes and ships have disappeared when traveling across the "Bermuda Triangle."

I haven't the faintest shred of hard evidence, only my psychic impressions, but I'm convinced he was taken from us by a flying saucer, a UFO. Whether or not he would be returned, I couldn't say. Why, exactly, he was taken, I don't know. Nevertheless, this was my conclusion.

What struck me most about the experience was the bizarre energy force I had briefly contacted. There was nothing normal about it, nothing human, nothing earthly. It both fascinated me and disturbed me.

I made contact with this energy a second time on October 3, 1969. I remember the date specifically because it happened during a radio broadcast. This was the time I made the prediction that Apollo 13 would suffer an explosion, yet the astronauts would return safely. I named "a magnetic field NASA isn't aware of" as the cause of the explosion. In truth, I saw something more than that. I saw the spacecraft intersecting a column of light extending upward from the earth, terminating somewhere in space.

This column of light, I perceived psychically, was some kind of extraterrestrial communications link. Whether it was ancient or modern, abandoned or in use, I couldn't say. But I somehow knew it was enormously powerful. I knew that any spacecraft that touched it would be damaged.

Apollo 13 was very nearly destroyed. Tapes of the astronaut's transmissions to the Houston Space Center at the time contain references to "a column of light" and "some kind of beam" but these comments were ignored in NASA's later analysis of the accident— or at least they were ignored in the report made public.

Later, I had occasion to discuss what I had perceived with Edgar Mitchell, the U.S. astronaut interested in psychic phenomena. It was at the Jersey Society of Parapsychology, Inc., after he addressed one of its meetings.

"Has NASA decided to route other spacecraft away from the light beam?" I asked.

Mitchell looked at me intently, without answering.

"I'm talking about the column of light that caused the Apollo 13 accident. I saw it psychically, some months before."

"You saw a column of light?"

"That's right. When I predicted the Apollo 13 disaster. I hope NASA knows about it now."

"I don't have anything to say about that," Mitchell said quickly. Before I had a chance to question him further, he'd turned his eyes away from me and started answering someone else's question.

I next made contact with the strange energy source on a trip to England. Like many tourists, I went to Stonehenge. I knew a little about it—that it seemed to be some sort of celestial calendar, that the ancients who'd built the place had floated the huge stones from a considerable distance. I'd also read that archaeologists were certain it had been used for sacrifice—but couldn't understand why their diggings had revealed no bones.

When I got there, I walked around among the stones. There was definitely something odd about the place. I could *feel* it, sense it. It was that same weird energy.

I found myself a quiet spot, sat down, closed my eyes, and attempted to project backward in time, to Stonehenge's origins.

It took an extraordinarily long time for the images to form in my mind. And they were somewhat jumbled at first. Finally, I was fully out-of-body. I believe I saw a kind of religious ceremony taking place among the stones. People wearing animal skins and coarsely woven cloth were moving in some sort of formal order, and chanting. Even today, I can recall the chanting. I'd rarely heard anything so beautiful.

Unfortunately, the language was not translated for me. But I could see what was going on. Using the "heel stone" as a kind of beacon, a huge, smooth, spherical shape floated out of the sky. It landed on top of the Stonehenge structure, which fit it perfectly.

My vision then faded, but fragments and psychic impressions continued to come through. The images told me that the builders of Stonehenge were an unusually advanced tribe of human beings. Their consciousness was greater than that of other nearby tribes. Creatures—they appeared to me as people—from other planets had made contact with this tribe.

My sense of it was that these extraterrestrial beings were dying out, that their bloodline was coming to an end. They were looking for another people with which to merge, a vigorous race who would give them new life. And that was the purpose of the contact. These beings caused the tribe to build Stonehenge, as both a landing platform and an altar.

The tribe prayed at Stonehenge, offering their minds and hearts to the creatures, whom they perceived as supreme beings. But it was a bloodless sacrifice—which is why no bones have ever been found.

In the end, the union failed and the creatures left. I don't know what became of the tribe that had built Stonehenge. Perhaps they also dispersed.

I suppose many would call all of this a fairy tale, a daydream. It may have been. Certainly, I have no evidence—other than my own memories—to back up what I've said. Accept it as an interesting story, if you must.

As for me, I am convinced the vision was true and accurate. One thing, especially, convinced me this is so: the same energy I'd sensed when I astral-projected to try to find that missing boy was present at Stonehenge.

In the summer of 1972, I once again came into contact with this energy force—this time directly. It began when a friend told me of some strange people, who'd been seen in New Mexico near a major experimental government installation.

These people—three men—had been seen on many occasions near this installation. Local residents said the men had been there for years—ever since the first experimental atomic explosion at Alamogordo in 1945.

"What's strange about the men?" I asked.

"Well," said my friend, "they just don't look quite right. You can't put your finger on it. It's more like they're imitation human beings."

"Don't you have anything more specific?"

"Most people think there's something wrong with their eyes, I don't know anything more than that."

At any rate, arrangements were made for me to fly to New Mexico and try to make contact with one of these individuals. The parties who made these arrangements wanted to have my psychic impressions of these people—if that's what they were.

And so I flew to New Mexico. The plan was for me to frequent a diner at which the men had often been seen. The confrontation came almost immediately. I walked into the diner, along with a man who'd seen the people in question and could identify them. He scanned the room, then drew me aside.

"That's one of them," he said, pointing as discreetly as possible.

I followed the gesture. My informant had singled out a man sitting at the end of the counter.

"All right," I said, "I'll take it from here."

I took a seat at the counter a few empty stools away from the man who'd been pointed out to me and tried to think of a way to approach him, to engage him in conversation so I could get some impression of him.

Finally, I looked his way, about to ask him to pass the sugar. Our eyes met. A tremendous vibration went through me. It was that same strange energy I had felt at Stonehenge, when I had sensed the Apollo 13 accident, when I had "located" the missing boy.

For a few seconds, our eyes held. I'd never seen any eyes like his before or since. They were like Bette Davis' eyes—only in reverse. Where hers pop out, his popped in, if you can imagine that. During our eye contact, I heard him speak to me, in my mind:

"Why have you come here? Why do you do this? You are just like one of us."

As I heard these words, all desire to speak to him left me. I got up from my seat and left the diner—to the intense disappointment of those who'd arranged the trip. But I could do nothing else.

I don't know if this man was from another planet. I don't know who he was or what he was. All I know is that I felt that bizarre energy again, and that I got a message from him.

In all, it was one of the strangest experiences in my life. Since then, I understand, none of the three men have been seen in the area again.

In November 1973, I again came into contact with this strange energy. The occasion was for my appearance on the TV program "To Tell the Truth." While at NBC I met Charles Hickson, a guest. He is the man who said he'd been taken aboard a flying saucer.

When I shook hands with Mr. Hickson, I felt this same energy pass through me. There was something different about the man, as if he had been changed by his experience. Hickson said he'd been fishing with a friend when they spotted a UFO. His fishing partner passed out and he was taken aboard, examined, then released. He told his story to the press, then, later, repeated it under hypnosis, in even more detail.

Something similar happened to a woman named Betty Hill, who wrote about her experiences in a book called *Interrupted Journey*. I met her once and she emanated the same sort of energy. We talked about her captors and her description closely resembled the man I'd seen in the diner.

I myself have never been contacted by a UFO. But I did see one once, in Maine. I am convinced such things are more than optical illusions and that they're the product of intelligent beings.

I suppose it's not out of the question—especially if I keep tracking down strange people—that I will be contacted some day. So be it.

Three Days of Darkness

During my lifetime, I've made thousands of predictions and forecasts. I could never hope to count them all.

But I've made only one prophecy.

The difference? As I see it, predictions or forecasts may involve only one person. At most, they refer to events affecting a few hundred. A prophecy, on the other hand, has significance for nations, continents, or even the entire planet.

My prophecy involves the future of mankind.

The vision began to take shape in my mind in October 1967, when I was at Catholic University in Washington. I was relaxing with some friends when the words came to me. I recognized their psychic nature and spoke them as I received them, as usual.

"Look to the heavens," I said. "The world will see strange phenomena in the days to come. There will be three days of darkness. The whole world shall see this. It shall be a sign for all. It shall be a warning . . ."

The words stopped coming.

"Do you know what you said?" one of my friends asked me.

I hadn't fully absorbed the content of what I'd repeated. "Yes, " I said. "This is the way many of my predictions come to me—spontaneously, at any time or place."

"That was no prediction," said another friend. "That was a prophecy."

Someone else remarked, "It certainly was not you speaking. I felt weird. You should have seen yourself. For a moment, your eyes were deeply fixed and penetrating. It was as if you were somewhere else."

By now, I was very uncomfortable. Everyone seemed to be waiting for me to say more, to add to my prophecy. But I had nothing more to say. There was a long, awkward silence. Then I changed the subject, if only to break the tension.

This vision disturbed and perplexed me more than any other psychic experience. I continued to question myself about it.

In 1972 I went to Paris. I visited the Chapel of the Apparitions. It was here that the Blessed Mother appeared to Sister Catherine Laboure several times and assigned her the task of having a Miraculous Medal made. The chapel still, to this day, holds the nun's incorrupt body preserved only by a glass case. The chapel also contains the chair where the Blessed Mother sat.

In the chapel, there is a motto inscribed: "Whatever you shall pray for, it shall be given to you." There was a statue of Mary there, surrounded by twelve electric lights.

Looking at the statue, I began thinking of the beautiful lady dressed in blue that some people had seen kneeling behind me, praying. Perhaps here, I thought, I would learn more.

Silently, I asked the Blessed Mother a question: "Is this vision about three days of darkness a genuine one?"

A voice answered me, inside my head. It said, "The three days of darkness are near. The eleventh hour has ended. The twelfth hour has begun." At that instant, the eleventh light of the twelve lights circling the statue blinked out.

I hadn't asked for a sign, but I believe I'd been given one.

As time passed, I was told more and more about what was coming. One day, I had another series of psychic images, a mixture of words and pictures, all of which seemed to relate to the three days of darkness.

If the warning is not heeded, I was told, there will be a holocaust before the year 2000. In this holocaust, people will die and cities will be destroyed. The whole world will be affected.

This is what came to me. But whether this is a picture of things to come or a symbolic vision, I do not know.

I decided—somewhat reluctantly, since it was so disturbing—to make the prophecy public, both parts of it. I revealed what I had seen to the Manchester, New Hampshire, *Union Leader* and to Henry Gosselin, editor of *Church World*. Both papers published reports of my vision and other papers picked up these reports.

Thereafter, I was asked about the prophecy each time I lectured.

"When is it going to happen?" I was asked by a woman in Manchester, New Hampshire.

"I've been told we'll see signs of its approach," I said. "There will be great natural catastrophies, an assassination attempt on the Pope, an intensification of the drug problem. Abortion will be legalized. Mercy killing will come to be accepted, both for the senile and for deformed children.

"Since we've already had most of those signs, I believe the three days of darkness will come soon."

"Well," the woman continued, "will science be able to explain what happens?"

"Yes," I said. "People will be able to explain the phenomena scientifically; they'll be able to make rational statements about why it happened. But they'll be missing the point. The three days of darkness will be a warning from God, not simply a freak of nature."

A man stood up. "What are we being warned about?"

"I believe the three days of darkness are intended to remind us of the value of life. Man is losing respect for life and three days of darkness is a warning that the trend must change."

At Cape Elizabeth, an Italian woman asked, "Does the prophecy mean the sun will lose its light for three days?"

A man asked, "Will it be an eclipse?"

My answer to both questions was the same: "I don't know. I suppose it could be, but I haven't been told."

In Van Buren, Maine, I was asked if my prophecy had anything to do with the Church.

"I believe so. The whole theme of my vision, as I see it, is the unity of the Church—and the unity of all men, for that matter."

As I'd feared, many people were worried by my prophecy of a holocaust. I'd asked my psychic self about the holocaust again and again, of course. The images I received confused me. One time, I had a vision of smoke rising over America. The vision was accom-

panied by a woman's voice, saying, "Because you have been dedi-
cated to me, I shall not destroy you completely."

In my vision, it seemed to me as though cities had been destroyed
and leveled. But I am not sure whether or not this was a symbolic
comment or a precise picture of the future. And other images seem
to say that the holocaust will not destroy the world, that it will just
be a powerful amplification of the warning implicit in the three
days of darkness. Frankly, I don't know whether millions will die or
few. To this day, I have not been given a specific answer.

Naturally, people questioned me closely about the holocaust. And
their questions prodded my psychic self.

"This holocaust," a woman asked, "is it some kind of world
catastrophe?"

"If you mean a world war, the answer is no." That much I was
sure of. The holocaust was an act of God, not of men.

"Do you think it may involve Russia and China?" asked a man.

"I do not think so."

The best question, I think, came in Van Buren, in a private conversation with a friend.

"How do you feel about your prophecy?" my questioner asked.

"I have no fear. It is certainly not a world war or the end of the
world. I feel it is a turning point for the Church and the world. To
me, this is a great sign of unity. It will bring the Church and the
people together. It is also the affirmation to the world that God is
with us."

I have since found out I'm not the only person to have visions of
three days of darkness. Others have made similar prophecies, some
of them dating back hundreds of years. More recently, Jeane Dixon
made a similar prediction.

A couple of years ago, someone sent me a pamphlet describing
the "Mystery of Garabandal," a series of apparitions that had appeared to four preteen Spanish girls on various dates in 1961 and
1962. I could hardly believe my eyes as I read the pamphlet. The
similarities between my vision and what the girls had said were astonishing.

On October 18, 1961, for example, one of the girls reported that
the Holy Mother had said, "If we do not amend our lives, there will
come a great chastisement." This had been said before, at Fatima.

But what followed was fresh.

The girl said Our Lady had warned her that all mankind would receive a heavenly warning, directly from God, "visible to the whole world," wherever anyone happened to be.

This warning, she went on, would provoke tremendous fear and self-reflection on our sins. And, if we ignored it, the whole world would be punished, as Our Lady had announced.

Because it came via the direct intervention of God, the girl went on, the punishment would be more terrifying and horrible than anything that had happened within memory.

To my astonishment, the pamphlet went on to say that the girls' visions were accompanied by all sorts of strange happenings: levitation, numbness to burns and blows, *visual immunity to the bright TV and movie spotlights* to which the girls were exposed, knowledge of languages, *mind reading, healing of various diseases and injuries,* such as cancer, leukemia, paralysis, and others.

Was this also mere coincidence? I do not know.

Toward an Understanding of Psychic Phenomena

I've often said I don't know how I accomplish my psychic feats, that I have no explanation for any of the wide variety of psychic experiences I've had over the years.

This is true—at least on one level. The actual mechanism behind my paranormal deeds is as much a mystery to me as it must be to everyone else. And the mystery is deepened by the fact that during these experiences, I have no extraordinary physical or mental sensations (though some people I've healed have reported tingling or vibrating sensations).

The psychic images and messages I receive come to me in a manner familiar to everyone, I think. They are sent via my stream of consciousness—the words and pictures that run through my mind quite naturally.

Everyone has this stream of consciousness to one degree or another, from what I understand. We're all engaged in constant internal conversation with ourselves. We all have moments when we watch internal movies in our mind's eye. From everything I've been able to discover, my stream of consciousness is no different from anyone else's—superficially anyhow.

And yet it is different, quite obviously. At certain times, it tells me things about the past, present, and future I couldn't otherwise know. It provides visual images of other places and other times, which I have evidently visited in some psychic way. This difference lies not in the apparent character of my stream of consciousness, but in its source and content.

I suppose most people think of their streams of consciousness as an integral part of their minds, a kind of behind-the-scenes thought factory, from which they select words and actions, for use on the outside. Most of the time, that's the way I think of my stream of consciousness.

But not always. When I approach it for psychic information, I think of it as a kind of internal voice, almost another self, a separate self. Since I know nothing of the character or personality of this internal voice, I call it "it." In a reading, for example, I'm likely to tell my subject, "Well, it told me that . . ." or "It said to me that . . ."

Most often, "it" speaks to me in response to questions. Sometimes "it" supplies images or thoughts in the form of hunches, intuitions, or premonitions. "It" is the part of me that travels when I have OB experiences—or at least "it" is what brings back reports of these experiences.

Like everyone else, I have daydreams and fantasies. I make guesses and estimates. I follow a train of logic to its conclusion. But somehow, the thoughts that flit through my mind as a result of these processes aren't the same as those provided by "it." When "it" tells me something, I usually have a very positive feeling about the information, a certitude.

Incidentally, my logical processes are prone to interfere with messages from "it," if I let them. That's why, when I ask my mind psychic questions, I must accept the first thought that comes into my head. If I think about the question, what comes will be the product of thinking, not of my internal voice.

Thus, the harder I try, the more I concentrate, the more important it is to me to receive a psychic message or commit a psychic act, the less likely it is that I'll succeed. My best work has always been done very casually, off the top of my head, so to speak, or at least very relaxed.

But these are subtle distinctions. So are the differences between my ordinary stream of consciousness—the one that governs my day-to-day activities—and the internal voice behind my psychic acts. I usually have a certitude about psychic messages, but not always. I usually know when a hunch is nothing more than a hunch, but not always.

So, to my dismay, I make mistakes—plenty of them. And there are other reasons for these mistakes—but I'm getting ahead of my story.

I've often wondered about the source of my internal voice. It seems incredible to me that the psychic impressions I receive are intended for me and me alone. There are millions of people more worthy. I can't believe that psychics and only psychics, among all human beings, have been singled out for instruction and illumination.

On the other hand, I am convinced that my psychic images and messages originate with some unknown source—some higher source I might say—if I were to put it in a religious light. And I believe my ability to hear this internal voice is God-given. But then, I believe all human qualities and aptitudes are God-given.

Over the years, I've developed a theory to explain—in the most general terms—my paranormal abilities. I have no evidence for the theory, except that it seems to fit the observed facts. It seems to account not only for all sorts of psychic phenomena, but also for many ordinary events about which most of us have wondered at one time or another.

It is my belief that there are strata of energy in the universe, so far undetected by scientific instruments. Please note, I said, "so far." Someday, maybe soon, I think science will find a way to detect this energy, just as it found ways to detect X rays, ultrasonic sound, and other energy forms.

I am convinced there is nothing supernatural or mystic about this energy or force. It is governed by physical laws, just as the transmission of television transmission signals, say, is governed by physical laws. But these laws have not yet been discovered. Until they are, we must build our knowledge of this energy on circumstantial and empirical evidence.

It is my hypothesis that this energy carries knowledge with it—as do the signals transmitted from a television station. I think it can pick up thoughts, information, other energy, even segments of a person's consciousness and transmit these back and forth through time and space.

It is also my hypothesis that human beings—*all human beings*—are able to pick this energy out of the other, just as condensers in radios or TV sets pick up transmission signals. But the energy affects each person in a different way, according to his or her character, personality, upbringing, interests, mental and physical abilities, environment, etc.

My name for this force is Creative/Perceptive Energy, or CPE. I suppose any other name would do as well. If I were writing only for a Catholic audience, I might call CPE grace, or the spiritual force. But I do not believe it has any special religious value, at least no more than anything else.

I call this force Creative/Perceptive Energy because I believe it is the power behind man's creative and perceptive acts, the explanation of inspiration, the vitality that prods men to be all they can possibly be, even to transcend themselves.

I have said CPE is external, that it is a kind of universal energy or spiritual force. But it can be perceived as an internal force too, depending how you look at it. I believe that CPE comes to us from outside ourselves, but that we use it as though it were a personal possession, as we use our other talents and energies. So I speak of people being in touch with CPE. However, I might just as well talk of a person using his or her CPE.

The way I see it, Creative/Perceptive Energy is what makes man move forward, what makes a man paint a great painting, create a great symphony, write a great book, establish a great relationship, become a great salesman, become a great athlete, or simply enjoy life to its fullest.

Have you ever wondered why, in the case of two men with apparently equal advantages, one is successful and the other a failure? I believe it's because one has tapped into the CPE in the universe and used it to his best advantage and the other hasn't. Have you ever wondered what makes some people magnetic, charismatic? I think it's because they are exceptionally attuned to CPE.

The man who is successful—be he doctor, builder, politician, or gardner—is very much in touch with CPE. The man who fails—at his job, in his relationships with others, even in his acceptance of himself—is not attuned to CPE, for the most part.

Of course, most people are in touch with CPE on some occasions but not others. Correspondingly, they do well at their chosen tasks at some times and badly at others.

When a person is not in touch with CPE, according to my way

of thinking, he is troubled, nervous, aggravated, upset. If he is out of touch more often than not, he's likely to be neurotic and unhappy. If he's out of touch almost always, he's likely to be depressed, even suicidal.

When a person is in touch with CPE, I believe, he is self-confident, happy, productive, at peace with himself. If he's in touch with it most of the time, he's likely to be outstanding at whatever he attempts. He's likely to be a well-realized, well-fulfilled individual. If he's in touch with it almost always, he's very probaby a genius in one or more of his endeavors.

Of course, almost no one is so firmly in touch with CPE that he makes no mistakes, has no failures. Even a great concert pianist, for example, a man who is extraordinarily well attuned to CPE, can have off nights, make mistakes. The same is true of the superathlete or supersalesman.

But over the long run, it is clear to all that something about these people lifts them above average, that they are extraordinarily able to use the abilities they have. It doesn't matter if the great pianist plays a piece badly from time to time, or if the great basketball player misses all his shots on occasion, or if the supersalesman comes up empty-handed during one sales trip.

So it is with the psychic. I use CPE to help me predict, heal, project light, travel out-of-body, etc. But like most everyone else, I am not always in touch with this energy force. And when I am not, I fail. My predictions look like nothing more than bad guesswork, I am unable to heal, light balls do not appear in my hands—no matter how hard I try, I cannot leave my body. I have moods, slumps.

But, over the long run, I've had an extraordinary and unexpected number of successes in predictions, healing, and the other psychic arts I practice. When examined this way—over a period of time—my psychic abilities are quite obvious, I believe.

Unfortunately, many people I come into contact with are not willing to look at the long run. I've faced audiences, or been on TV programs, or even confronted individuals who wanted an instant demonstration of my powers. If, for some reason, I couldn't perform as requested, these people not only disbelieved my abilities, they dismissed the entire field of psychic phenomena.

It's as though a great pianist or a great athlete were given a single chance to demonstrate, beyond any doubt, his remarkable prowess. Under those conditions, I can imagine Vladimir Horowitz playing badly, Walt Frazier missing seven shots out of ten, Billie Jean King double-faulting three times in a row, or Bobby Fisher getting himself checkmated.

And my problem is even more complicated than theirs. The mechanisms behind most skills, be they physical or intellectual, are well known. They can be analyzed, then practiced. When mistakes are made, these, too, can be analyzed, then corrected.

Unfortunately, no one knows the exact mechanism of the skill behind psychic phenomena. In a sense, when a psychic makes a prediction, it's like a blind man trying to draw a picture. Because he does not understand—or in the case of the blind man, see—exactly what he is doing, because he cannot use his skills with any degree of control, he often fails.

If a blind man could draw a picture eight times out of ten, however, all would be satisfied that he had a very unusual talent. I only wish that psychics were judged the same way. My own personal batting average in my predictions, as I figure it, is about 85 per cent. I wish skeptics would concentrate on my successes, not my failures. I'm not a magician. If I were, I'd be successful 100 per cent of the time.

But I realize that many people—perhaps most—find it difficult and threatening to accept any psychic phenomena as real. They have a heavy emotional investment in disbelief, for to disbelieve what they cannot understand is to reaffirm belief in the world as they see it.

If all human beings are affected—in one way or another—by CPE, you might wonder why psychic abilities are not a universal skill. Someday, they may be. I strongly believe the potential is there. The reason most people aren't psychic is social, not a matter of physics or biology.

Most people cannot tap into CPE to know the future, to travel out-of-body, to heal, etc., simply because they're convinced these things are impossible—for them, at least. That's why most people can't paint, write, or compose music, by the way. They firmly believe such things are beyond their capability. So naturally, they are.

This isn't so much the fault of the individual, but of society. Our society—mainly through our families—teaches that psychic phenomena are imaginary, unreal. And it is our families, I fear, who teach us that we cannot paint, write, compose, or whatever.

Most people are introduced to these ideas when they are still very young children, when they have no information of their own that runs contrary to what they're being told. So most people accept the information given them by their families without question.

My family, as I've related, fully accepted the paranormal. Their open-mindedness on the subject allowed me to be open-minded too. And before I was old enough to "know better," I was tapping CPE in the service of my psychic abilities. At least in my formative years, I was brought up with a positive view of psychic phenomena.

Of course, I use CPE for other things, too. In addition to being a psychic, I am a psychologist, a counselor, a composer, philosopher, a painter, and a theologian. I use CPE as much as I can in all of these fields, and in my interpersonal relationships too. There's nothing so special about this. Whoever taps into this energy source can use it as he will.

Despite our society's widespread disbelief in the paranormal, I am convinced that a great many people have frequent psychic experiences, usually without knowing it.

Have you ever had a hunch—the right hunch? Did you ever experience an extraordinary coincidence? Have you ever had a dream come true? Were you ever—luckily—in exactly the right place at the right time? Did you ever think of someone, then have him call? Did you ever wish for something and have your wish granted? Have you ever had a sudden inspiration that solved a problem. If so, maybe you're more psychic than you're willing to admit.

Beyond experiences like these, I believe many people use their CPE psychically, though they wouldn't describe it that way. This happens when people choose the right marriage partner, or the right job, or the right place to live. Artists and writers make psychic decisions when they choose the right subject or the right approach. So do doctors when they make a difficult diagnosis, or businessmen when they make the right business decision, or investors, when they fortunately choose the right investment.

Whenever people surpass themselves, whenever they draw on

resources they didn't know they had, whenever they go beyond logic to make their lives better, or more successful, or more fulfilled, they're acting psychically, they're tapping Creative/Perceptive Energy.

At the moment, this is the best explanation I have for the strange things I do and the strange things I experience. I hope to build on it in the future. I hope others will build on it.

How to Tap
Your Own Psychic Powers

Nothing would please me more than to see many thousands of people begin to undertake their own journeys into the psychic realm as a result of this book.

It would please me because it would advance men and women another step toward the full realization of the powers to which they are heir. It would bring closer that day when people are fully in touch with themselves and with others. It would, I am firmly convinced, increase the amount of love, peace, and understanding in the world.

I would also be gratified if, through reading this book, many are encouraged to make their own psychic explorations, because I can think of no better way to share my gift and to discharge the obligations that came with it.

For these reasons and because I am convinced all people—at least potentially—are psychic, I want to take the next pages to teach, as well as I can, how others might develop their powers.

Over the years, I've developed several concepts to lead others toward psychic experiences. They are disarmingly simple, but they've succeeded on literally hundreds of occasions, with hundreds of different people.

Rule one: Allow yourself to believe. No one ever learned to do something he "knew" was impossible. If you disbelieve, in principle, either you will deny the validity of any psychic experience you may have or you simply may not permit yourself to have such an experience.

In my experience, committed disbelievers rarely have psychic experiences, though they may be affected by the psychic abilities or experiences of others. For instance, I've found I could give readings, make predictions, diagnose, and even heal disbelievers.

Skeptics are another matter. Those who haven't made up their minds in advance of the facts are good subjects for psychic experience. I've had frequent successes with skeptics, leading a number of them to repeated psychic experiences. Naturally, those who already accept the paranormal are most easily taught to experience it for themselves.

Rule two: Place no judgment on the paranormal. Psychic experiences are neither the work of the devil nor evidence of divinity. They are, I believe, as natural as athletic ability or facility with words or numbers. There is no more reason to be frightened about having a psychic experience than there is reason to fear making an extraordinary tennis shot, or adding up a column of figures in your head or writing a poem.

My point: there is nothing supernatural about psychic experiences. On the contrary, they are quite natural. Someday, I am sure, science will be able to explain the paranormal as easily as it now explains how your television set can pick up a picture or how your auto engine can move your car at fifty miles an hour.

Since there is nothing supernatural about psychic experiences, there is no reason for fear when you have one. You will not be attacked by spirits from the netherworld. Witches will not descend down your chimney. You will not lose your mind.

The same is true if someone you know has a psychic experience. That person has not made a pact with the devil (nor has he benefited from angelic aid). He's no more bewitched, cursed, weird, or even wonderful than he was before. He's just learned to use a part of himself that was formerly dormant.

Rule three: Identify your previous psychic experiences. Rare is the person who hasn't had some kind of paranormal event in his life, at one time or another, however he might label it. What kind have you had?

Have you known someone was going to telephone you—an instant before he did? Have you known someone was going to pay you an unscheduled visit? Do you often experience *déjà vu*, the intense feeling that you've been someplace before, heard something before, seen something before—though you couldn't have?

Do you often have hunches about important events, hunches that turn out to be remarkably accurate? Do your dreams sometimes come true? Are you forever meeting people you know in unexpected places? Do you win more often than would be expected at raffles or in lotteries? Do you have an unusually well-developed "card sense"?

Do you always find a parking place in front of wherever you're going? Do you always seem to come up with tickets to sold out events (after someone fortunately cancels out)? When you play golf (or tennis or baseball or whatever) does your ball always take a lucky hop? Do you often know what someone is going to say before they say it?

What I am suggesting here is that you carefully review all of your own experiences, looking for those which might be paranormal. If you can identify an area in which you have had several unusual experiences, so much the better.

This area is where you should begin, when you start your personal psychic journey. You will work on it until you have confidence and facility, then begin to broaden your approach to include other facets of the paranormal.

If no particular area stands out, or if you have several of ap-
psychometry, a psychic art which involves touching an object
and by touch alone receiving information normally available only
parently equal value, I recommend that you start where I did—with
through other means. This is what I did at the age of eighteen
months, when I touched the edges of stacked records and picked
out my favorite again and again, though it was somewhere in the
middle.

Rule four: Relax, take it easy. Psychic feats are easy, when they're properly performed. And you must treat them as easy.

When you try too hard, when you bring in your mental artillery—your imagination, your logic, your concentration, your knowledge of the situation or of the world—you'll fail.

I believe psychic powers lie at the top of the mind, so to speak. This is a layer most of us pass through and ignore with every thought. We almost always operate on more complex levels.

Learning to be psychic involves, at its core, learning to operate on the simplest levels, learning to accept the first images and impressions that flood your mind, instead of delving deeper.

If there is any one barrier to mastering the paranormal, it is the almost overwhelming temptation to go deeper, to wait for more certainty, to try to pin down a thought or an image in more ways than one, by using the mind's other powers.

As aware of this pitfall as I am, I often fall into it. When I do, I tend to brush off genuinely psychic impressions as having no value or significance. That's when my performance drops off. When I catch myself and begin trusting my very first impressions, I do much better.

I cannot stress relaxation and faith in first impressions too strongly. If you cannot relax, if you are unwilling to accept the initial images that flit through your mind, your psychic experiences will be few and far between, coming only when you are completely off guard. In this frame of mind, the harder you try to have a psychic experience, the smaller your chance of success.

Rule five: Give yourself easy tasks at first; gradually increase the difficulty. One of my favorite ways to introduce a person to psychic experience is to give him a pack of cards.

"All right," I say, "cut the cards. But before you cut them, feel their edges. Don't concentrate, don't push. Feel easily and quickly. Cut the deck to a jack, ace, or five."

"Any one of three cards?" my subject usually asks.

"Exactly. Give yourself twelve chances out of fifty-two. When you develop facility you can cut down later, to eight chances out of fifty-two, then four out of fifty-two."

What do I mean, "feel the edges"? Here we get into that part of the paranormal that doesn't fit easily into words. I mean that when you feel the edges of a deck of cards, "looking" for a jack, an ace, or a five, something will tell you you're touching the card in question. In some manner—the exact mechanism isn't known to anyone —you'll get a signal from your fingers that this is it.

Here's another psychometric exercise that will illustrate my point. Take a deck of cards and hold it face down. Rub your fingers over the backs of each card, briefly, until you get an impression of its face color—red or black. After psychically declaring the color, look at the card. Place each card you "guessed" correctly in one pile, and each incorrect "guess" in another pile.

Now chance would dictate that each pile would be composed of twenty-six cards, at least over the long run. You may find this isn't so in your case. Some people consistently score higher than chance on this test, correctly identifying the color of thirty or more cards. Others score higher than chance, but in reverse, misidentifying thirty or more every time. Both sorts of scores are evidence of psychic activity.

When you work with cards this way (or attempt any psychic feat) you must not expect results at first, though that sometimes happens. In most people, the psychic skills are dormant and flabby, like a muscle that's never been exercised. You develop your psychic muscles in the same way you develop those in your arms and legs— you exercise.

Find a friend and practice. Lay out a task for yourself, such as the one I described. Variations of these tasks can be found in many places, such as in books about psychics, or books about the subject. Hemisphere Publications of Hollywood, Florida, puts out a booklet called *You and ESP*, which is filled with various ways to test your psychic ability. While I do not agree with everything said in this booklet, it will provide you with useful exercise. Another helpful book is David Hoy's *Psychic and Other ESP Party Games*. Two books by my friend Harold Sherman are also first-rate, *How to Make ESP Work for You* and *Harold Sherman's ESP Manual*.

If you are inclined toward psychometry and you develop some skill with the card exercises I've described, your next step is to attempt to sensitize yourself to other objects. Have a friend provide the personal effects of a third party, preferably someone unknown to you, and attempt to gain information about the person by merely touching or holding the object.

You can carry this even further by attempting readings; that is, by talking to people you're unacquainted with, holding their hands, and talking about the impressions that come to you.

If you trust your first impressions, the ones that come most easily to you, you'll soon be surprised at how often you're right.

Rule six: Gradually explore other psychic areas. Once you have achieved some skill at psychometry or whatever field you have chosen, try another, again starting with easy tasks, then expanding.

Take telepathy, for instance. Don't begin by trying to perceive an entire thought someone else is having. Instead, start with an envelope and five simple pictures—a mountain, a river, a house, a tree, a seashore.

While you are out of the room, your friend should take one of the five pictures and put it into an envelope. Then, when you return, you try to say which picture is in the envelope. Don't expect to do it every time. I can't, and I don't know of any other psychic who can. In fact, at the beginning, don't be surprised if you do no better than chance. (In this case, you should have one correct guess in every five trials.) But keep at it. If you've followed my other rules, you'll soon be guessing correctly an average of two or three times out of five.

Once you have mastered picture guessing to the point that you're consistently scoring above chance, move on to complicated telepathic work. Substitute five words for the pictures. When you begin achieving significant results with words, try sentences. Then, finally, if you prove adept, do some trials with no predetermined words or pictures. Let your partner put whatever word or picture he wishes into the envelope.

Another way to move to the more specific is to increase the odds against a correct chance answer. Take a piece of paper and divide it into a grid pattern of twenty-five squares. Make two copies. Have your friend mark one square while you are out of the room and seal his piece of paper in an envelope. When you return, you mark a square on your piece of paper. Then compare. According to chance, you should mark the same square one time in every twenty-five trials. Want to decrease the odds? Have him mark five squares, then mark five yourself.

Rule seven: Don't make limits for yourself. Once you've had some success, once you're able to produce results exceeding those expected by chance, try whatever psychic feats that appeal to you. Try predictions. Announce your premonitions to witnesses. Try psychic photography. Any feat any psychic has described is fair game. Read autobiographies such as this and attempt to duplicate the achievements described.

I'd make this same prescription for those who've failed at their first choice of psychic experiences. You can never be sure where your inclinations lie, in which areas you might be able to perform. If I hadn't experimented, I'd never have known I could project light balls into my hands. I'd never have known I could heal.

As long as you're interested and as long as you follow the other rules I've described, try whatever appeals to you. You have psychic abilities within you—I am sure of that. It's just a matter of letting them come out.

I wish I could list a dozen other rules, which, if followed religiously, would lead unerringly to psychic experiences. But I have no more rules and no more advice to offer. Further, the procedures I've described are enough. They work. I've used them to teach hundreds of people to tap their own personal psychic powers.

When I taught at St. John's University in Brooklyn, I once took an envelope, inserted a picture postcard, then sealed the envelope. I then passed it around the class and asked the students to feel the envelope and try to sense what picture was on the postcard, what colors predominated, what shapes they perceived, etc. The results were significant enough to show that something had happened, though just what was not clear. Either I was transmitting the picture to my students telepathically, or they were using abilities of their own.

Throughout my teaching career, I continued to assign my students psychic tasks from time to time. At Cheverus, I used a sheet of paper marked off with a grid of twenty-five squares. I had one student sit in one room, another student sit in a second room. Each had a copy of the grid.

I instructed one student to put his finger on one square. I told the other to pass his hand over the paper until he felt a heaviness. "Let your hand fall there," I said. "It is the square your 'sender' is touching."

In one trial, twenty students participated—ten as senders, ten as receivers. Each receiver-sender pair was given five chances. Nine times out of ten, the receiving student hit a bull's-eye. The tenth receiver put his finger on the square immediately adjacent to the one on which the sender had his finger.

Another time, I tried to identify those among my students who were sensitive to telepathic reception. I opened a book at random and picked out a single word. The first word I chose was "Freud." I asked my students to write down the word I'd selected—without telling them what it was, of course. Six students got it. I then picked another word—"grape." This time seven got it.

To me, this is just more evidence of how widespread psychic abilities really are.

Later, one of my students asked me to find a ring he'd lost some three months earlier.

"Why don't you try yourself?" I asked.

"Psychically?"

"Certainly."

So he sat in his seat, relaxed, and thought about the ring. Suddenly, a picture flashed through his mind, a spot in his house. The next day in class, he was wearing his ring. It had been exactly where he'd pictured it.

I've even taught some people how to tap their psychic abilities while on radio or television. I'll let Craig Worthing describe a couple of incidents of this nature in which he was personally involved:

"The first live television show Dr. Tanous did was back in Portland, Maine. On the night before, he appeared on my radio program. Alex, another man, and I were in the room. 'There are certain things you can do to test your psychic abilities,' Alex said.

"He started telling me, 'Feel the edge of these cards and think about the jack or the ace and think about it and think about it, and all of a sudden, your fingers will pick it. Don't think twice, cut it where your fingers tell you to.'

"So Alex did it seven or eight times. And I said, 'My God!' The other person in the room then did it five times out of six. I thought, 'This is crazy.' You know, we had shuffled the cards each time. Then I went ten for ten myself. It was almost as though the cards seemed to enlarge when your fingers touched them.

"So the next day, we did the TV show. And I said, why don't we test it with the boys—my twin sons. The boys were scared about appearing on television. So were Alex and I—it was our first time. Well, Alex pulled out the deck of cards and told the kids how to do it. Damned if they didn't pick a jack or ace five times out of five tries."

Craig and I often talked about how one might use his psychic abilities to win at gambling or horse racing. I knew I could never use my gift for personal gain. If I did, it would be taken from me. But I couldn't think of any reason Craig shouldn't try. So I told him what to do. It wasn't until some time later that he tried what I'd suggested. The results were remarkable. Here's how he tells the story:

"I know nothing about race tracks, but I've always kidded people about the Alex Tanous method of betting. That's when you go to the track and you get the little booklet that lists all the races and all the horses in them. You take this booklet and scan the page. Alex says, 'Don't use much time, just scan down. And the first name that jumps out at you, that's the one who's going to win.'

"Sounds silly, I know, but listen to this: I went to Vernon Downs last year with a friend. It was one of the few times I'd been to a track. There were nine races that night. Using the Alex Tanous method, I went through the whole booklet in about two minutes, circling horses' names.

"My friend looked at my choices and he didn't believe them. He said, 'This one is six to one. You don't have a chance on this one. And this one is crazy.' He took quite a while going through his own booklet, handicapping his choices with care.

"Well, in the first five races, I had five first-place winners. In the other four, I had two seconds and a third. Only one horse I'd circled finished out of the money—and that one came in fourth.

"My friend—who didn't do nearly so well—couldn't believe it. And to tell you the truth, I thought it was uncanny myself."

I suppose you could say this was just luck—and maybe it was. But I don't think that word can be applied very easily on other occasions when I showed people how to tap their psychic abilities.

One striking example occurred in May 1974, just after I began work on this book with my collaborator, Harvey Ardman. Harvey, his wife, Perri, and I were sitting in his house one evening, discussing out-of-body experiences. I suggested we try an out-of-body experience then and there. I'll let Harvey tell what happened:

"Alex walked over to the bookshelf in the living room and pulled out one of those big cocktail-table museum books. It was part of a mail-order series. When it came, months earlier, I just stuck it up into the bookshelf without looking at it.

"Anyhow, Alex opened it up at random, face down. None of us could see which page he'd opened it to. He carried it into the guest room this way and put it on the guest bed, face down.

"Back in the living room, he asked Perri and me to sit back and relax and tell our minds to go into the guest room, take a look at the page to which the book was opened, then come back to our bodies. Then he would ask us to report on what we'd seen.

"Well, for about ten minutes or so, my mind was filled with the usual range of words and pictures. I concentrated on 'traveling' into the guest room—all the while thinking the whole thing was pretty ridiculous. In the tenth minute, Alex said, 'What did you see?'

"At that instant, there was a funny kind of picture in my mind. I described it: I said I saw only the lower left-hand corner of the page. It was entirely green, I said, and it was mottled, as if it were a copper roof. Diagonal lines ran from the corner up toward the top of the page.

"'Okay,' Alex said, 'now how about you, Perri?' Perri told him she'd seen some kind of round structure made of white brick. Alex then told what he'd seen: a brick house in a rural setting, with black posts. 'No,' he corrected himself, 'black trees. Trees painted black.' Perri and I looked at each other, smiled a little nervously, and shrugged.

"Then the three of us walked into the guest room and turned the book face up. As it happened, Alex had opened up the book to a two-page picture, a color photograph.

"Dominating the picture was a large white stone castle. In the background, one could see a white stone tower—a circular structure. In the foreground was a stand of trees. Their trunks were nothing more than silhouettes—they were entirely black.

"And in the lower left-hand corner was a stretch of lawn, green lawn. It had the mottled appearance of a copper roof. Diagonal lines of sunlight ran across it, starting at the bottom corner and running toward the top of the page, where the book was bound.

"What do I make of this? I don't know what to make of it. Every word that we said about the picture turned out to be completely accurate.

"It is possible, I suppose, that Alex looked at the picture before he put the book on the bed. Perri and I weren't there. But I know for sure I didn't look at the book. Neither did Perri. Not until we made our 'trips.' "

I can't explain it either, any better than I can explain a similar incident with another writer acquaintance, Dan Greenburg, and his friend, Melanie Turner. Here's how Dan describes it:

"Alex told me he could teach people to do various things, like astral projection. He said we could try an experiment. Did I have a picture book that I wasn't familiar with? I did. We went to the bedroom where the bookshelves are and he selected an old copy of *Horizon* magazine, which I hadn't looked at in a long time—if ever—and he opened it without looking at it, facing outward, and put it down on the bed.

"And then we went down to the living room. We turned down the lights and lay down on the floor, got comfortable, took off our shoes, closed our eyes, and Alex tried to relax us. He asked us to imagine that we were leaving our bodies and floating upstairs to the bedroom and up onto the bedspread and under the pages of the *Horizon* magazine and looking up—and what did we see?

"He asked me first. And I said, 'Well, I've got an image of a color photograph, on the dark side, with a lot of people in it. Then I said no, it was a color painting, of a religious nature, with a lot of people in it, dark colored, with a three-quarter inch white border around it and a glare on the page.'

"Then he asked Melanie and she said, 'I think I'm doing it wrong—I didn't get that at all.' And he said, 'Don't worry about that—tell me what you see.' And she said, 'I see a small black-and-white portrait of a woman with a broad-brimmed hat, with lots of white space around it and lots of type.'

"And then he said, 'Okay, I'll tell you what I see—I see very much what Dan described—a religious painting, dark colors, mostly blues and greens, in a style that most people wouldn't think was pleasant.'

"It turned out that the *Horizon* magazine—on the left-hand page —was exactly what Melanie had described, and on the right-hand page was exactly what Alex and I had described."

This isn't the only psychic experience I've shared with Melanie Turner, who works on NBC's "Monitor." The most interesting of these, perhaps, involves a silver bracelet she's worn.

One day, I used this bracelet as a psychometric object. I held it, rubbed it, and told her many things about her life and those she knew. The bracelet was one of those heavy silver ones, with a small opening at its bottom that allowed it to be slipped over the wrist.

Soon after I rubbed the bracelet, Melanie noticed that it appeared almost severed in two, at the top. As she tells it, it was severed in the spot toward which I had been rubbing, from both sides.

She took it to the jeweler, who said fixing it would be no problem, it would be stronger than before. He soldered the break with heavy silver.

A few days later, while she was sunbathing on the top of her apartment building, near the swimming pool, eating a popsicle, the bracelet suddenly fell from her wrist. She picked it up to find that both ends of the bracelet had been bent up toward the middle and this time, the bracelet was completely severed, as if it had been sawed.

"I knew it had to be Alex," she told her friends.

The out-of-body experiences of Harvey and Perri Ardman, and of Dan Greenburg and Melanie Turner reinforce one of my most strongly held convictions: that all people have psychic abilities, powers they can use under the proper conditions, given a minimum of instruction and encouragement, if only they allow themselves to believe.

Remember this: no one who never made a prediction ever had a prediction come to pass. No one who never looked into the future ever saw a moment beyond the present. No one who never attempted to heal ever brought someone back to health. No one who never had a dream ever had a dream come true.

My Faith
and My Psychic Self

Any psychic, or anyone who works in the area of psychic phenomena, must eventually ask himself how these apparently inexplicable events fit with his conception of the universe—not his scientific or rational conception, but his moral religious conception.

As a man with a strict Catholic upbringing and also a man who has been both attacked and defended by representatives of the Church for decades, I confronted this question early in life.

Did I—a man who performed remarkable feats of my own—believe in God? Was it possible for me to be a psychic and keep my faith? Could I accept the tenets of my religion and at the same time almost routinely surpass man's generally recognized abilities? Could I find support for my psychic self in my religion?

This questioning, this doubt, this struggle to plumb the depths of my beliefs, left me with a faith that is more profound and more strongly felt than before my self-examination.

My psychic experiences—far from driving me away from my faith—have reinforced my belief in a higher power. These events have given me the feeling that I have shared in something divine. I believe some force outside myself has filled me with splendor, with grace.

Christ is my greatest support, my greatest guide. He helped me in my period of doubt and he helps me now. Today, Christians regard Christ as the son of God. But he was a man as he lived. And, as a man, I consider him the greatest psychic the world has ever known.

Christ performed psychic feats almost without number. And as a result, he was condemned by the religious leaders of his day, as someone who worked with the devil. Modern-day psychics, myself included, have also been condemned from the pulpit on that basis.

I don't believe that I or any other psychic is divine, in the sense Christ is divine. But I believe my powers, like Christ's, are God-given. I believe God has given these gifts to all men, if only they would use them.

I believe that man is created in the image and likeness of Christ and I aspire to reach his level, not as a God of course, but as a man.

This thought is not unique to me. Christ himself believed his abilities were available to men. "These things I have done and greater things you shall do," he said.

And, at the Ecumenical Council, it was proclaimed that Christ's gifts would be given to the people. Pastors were told to watch for those members of their congregations who possessed such abilities. (The pentecostal and charismatic movements were inspired by this proclamation.)

Christ reached the highest state of consciousness available to men, and, in that state, performed astonishing psychic feats. Before his time and since, other men have achieved heightened states of consciousness and achieved similar deeds. The only difference is that Christ performed these feats to reveal his destiny.

But Christ is not my only guide. I take much strength from the Bible. I see the Bible—from its very first page—as a book of prophecies and dreams. Certainly, it is filled with examples of psychic phenomena. And Biblical figures saw these remarkable events as evidence in support of the existence of God, rather than the contrary. This is consonant with my own beliefs.

I also take inspiration from St. Augustine, who, I feel, was another great psychic. Yet I am a student of St. Thomas Aquinas, too. I see his logic and St. Augustine's psychic insights as complementary.

The writings of the great French theologian Pierre Teilhard de Chardin have also had a great influence on my thinking. I sometimes feel his words describe what I am living.

As a member of the Eastern Rite Catholic Church, the original Church of Christ, where the Mass is said in Christ's own language,

Aramaic, I have no difficulty embracing the tenets of my faith. I no longer see any conflict between my religious beliefs and my psychic self.

I was brought up, however, in a Western culture and exposed, from my earliest years, to the Roman Church. I have no trouble reconciling my psychic nature with the beliefs of the Roman Church either, but I see that church as being overburdened with rules and regulations, some of which make no sense to me whatever. Yet I follow them, since they were integral to my upbringing.

My religious problems, such as they are, do not involve the tenets of my faith. They center around certain churchmen, those who dismiss psychic phenomena out of hand, condemning or making fun of those who work in the field.

I would say to these churchmen, it's time to open up your eyes. It can no longer be disputed that psychic phenomena exist and that there are people who can perform psychic feats. To those churchmen who scoff, I recommend that they do a little research before they crawl out on a shaky limb.

I do want to make clear, however, that I am not addressing the Church in general. There are many priests who hold me and my work, and others like me, in the deepest respect.

After I was attacked from the pulpit and in *Church World*, a religious newspaper, Rev. Clement D. Thibodeau, among others, came to my defense.

He said that the Church previously failed "to distinguish between the natural phenomena and the occult. Today, there are serious efforts being made to establish the factual basis for the many astounding but undeniable phenomena once condemned as Black Magic. ESP is a fact."

I believe it is only a matter of time until all churchmen believe as does Reverend Thibodeau. And that day will bring with it the incredible flowering of psychic powers among all peoples that I hope for.

Toward the coming of that day, I offer this prayer:

> Lord,
> Let me do my thing;

It's not that we have
So much hate in the world,
As we have not yet
Learned how to love.

It is greater to receive
Than to give,
Because we cannot give
What we have not received;
And Lord,
You have given me so much!
Your Life-giving Spirit
And all of Your gifts;
If I use them well,
I hope for my reward.
If I misuse them,
I know my punishment.

Lord,
Let me do my thing.
Where there is darkness,
Let me bring Your light;
Where there is illness,
Your health;
Where there is despair,
Your faith, hope, and love.
Whatever it may be, Lord,
Let me do my thing.
And a small postscript for all of us,
Won't You teach us how to love
The world, the people, and You?
If we cannot love the world,
We cannot love one another,
And we can never learn to love You.

Our past we leave to Your mercy, Lord
Our present to Your love and Grace
Our future to Your destiny for us.
And we pray that within each of us

We'll find the love
That will bring the peace
You have promised,
For all things begin and end in love.

Alex Tanous